Consulting Authors

William C. Kyle, Jr.
E. Desmond Lee Family Professor of
  Science Education
University of Missouri—St. Louis
St. Louis, Missouri

Brenda Webb, Assistant Professor
Kilby Laboratory School
University of North Alabama
Florence, Alabama

Columbus, Ohio

The **McGraw·Hill** Companies

Program Reviewers

Kimberly Bailey
Teacher
Ariel Community Academy
Chicago, Illinois

Suzanne Giddens
Teacher
Jenks West Elementary
Jenks, Oklahoma

David Maresh
Teacher
Yucca Valley Elementary
Yucca Valley, California

M. Kate Thiry
Teacher
Wright Elementary School
Dublin, Ohio

April Causey Trull
Teacher
Bolivia Elementary School
Bolivia, North Carolina

Constance W. Zehner, M.S.
CZ Consulting
Houston, Texas

Assessment Specialist

Michael Milone, Ph.D.
Placitas, New Mexico

Cover Photo
Francois Gohier/Photo Researchers, Inc., (background) Franz Lanting/Minden Pictures

Acknowledgments
The publisher gratefully acknowledges permission to reprint science standards from the following:

National Science Education Standards, Copyright © 1996 by the National Academy of Sciences. Courtesy of the National Academy Press, Washington, D.C.

www.sra4kids.com

Copyright © 2004 by SRA/McGraw-Hill.

All rights reserved. Except as permitted under the United States Copyright Act, no part of this publication may be reproduced or distributed in any form or by any means, or stored in a database or retrieval system, without the prior written permission of the publisher, unless otherwise indicated.

Send all inquiries to:
SRA/McGraw-Hill
8787 Orion Place
Columbus, OH 43240-4027

Printed in the United States of America.

ISBN 0-07-572770-6

2 3 4 5 6 7 8 9 QPD 08 07 06 05

TABLE OF CONTENTS

Program Overview iv

Standards Correlation ix

Scope and Sequence xii

Writing Assessment xiv

Investigating Skills

Skill 1   **HOW TO Make and Use a Model**
Shaking in Your Shoes 2

Skill 2   **HOW TO Measure**
Using a Thermometer 4

Skill 3   **HOW TO Choose the Right Tool**
Making a Compost Pile 6

Skill 4   **HOW TO Make a Hypothesis**
Magnet Mysteries 8

Skill 5   **HOW TO Collect Data**
Think Fast! 10

Skill 6   **HOW TO Control Variables**
Changing How Plants Grow 12

Skill 7   **HOW TO Design an Experiment**
What Do Seeds Need? 14

Skill 8   **HOW TO Draw Conclusions**
Eugenie Clark Studies Sharks 16

Skill 9   **HOW TO Prepare an Observation Report**
Curious about Mold 18

Reading and Thinking Skills

Skill 10   **HOW TO Classify**
Machines Make Work Easier 20

Skill 11   **HOW TO Compare and Contrast**
Comparing the Planets 22

Skill 12   **HOW TO Determine Cause and Effect**
Fire! 24

Skill 13   **HOW TO Tell Fact from Opinion**
Coral Reefs 26

Skill 14   **HOW TO Find the Main Idea**
Nature's Recyclers 28

Skill 15   **HOW TO Take Notes**
Alternative Fuel-Powered Vehicles . . 30

Skill 16   **HOW TO Estimate**
One Serving, Please 32

Skill 17   **HOW TO Predict**
Erosion 34

Skill 18   **HOW TO Infer**
Leaves of Three, Let Them Be 36

Skill 19   **HOW TO Make a Decision**
Choosing a Science Fair Project . . . 38

Skill 20   **HOW TO Work in a Group**
Making a Terrarium 40

Writing and Research Skills

Skill 21 **HOW TO** Make a Learning Log
Life at the Vents 42

Skill 22 **HOW TO** Write a Paragraph
National Parks in Trouble 44

Skill 23 **HOW TO** Write an Outline
Natural Resources. 46

Skill 24 **HOW TO** Write a Summary
Are There Microbes in Your Future? 48

Skill 25 **HOW TO** Write a Description
Yellowstone's Hot Springs 50

Skill 26 **HOW TO** Write a Comparison/Contrast
Improving Technology Improves Health 52

Skill 27 **HOW TO** Write about a Process
Glass: A "Super Cool" Matter 54

Skill 28 **HOW TO** Use the Library
Volcanoes. 56

Skill 29 **HOW TO** Write a Report
Pedal Power 58

Skill 30 **HOW TO** Prepare a Display
Telescopes 60

Skill 31 **HOW TO** Do a Survey
Cleaning Up the Environment. 62

Chart and Graph Skills

Skill 32 **HOW TO** Read a Time Line
Rockets! 64

Skill 33 **HOW TO** Make a Table
Going, Going, Gone? 66

Skill 34 **HOW TO** Read a Bar Graph
Up in Smoke 68

Skill 35 **HOW TO** Make a Line Graph
Tracking the Temperature 70

Skill 36 **HOW TO** Read a Circle Graph
Conserving Water. 72

Skill 37 **HOW TO** Make a Diagram
Amazing Insects 74

Skill 38 **HOW TO** Read a Flowchart
How Storms Form 76

Skill 39 **HOW TO** Make a Graphic Organizer
A Bright Idea 78

Skill 40 **HOW TO** Read a Map
The Everglades. 80

Test-Taking Strategies

Skimming a Passage 82

Understanding Sequence 84

Making Comparisons 86

Skipping Difficult Questions 88

Using Keywords 90

Using Context 92

Working Carefully 94

Using Logic 96

Reduced Student Pages 100

Skills Workbook Answers 153

• INVESTIGATING • READING • WRITING • CHARTS • GRAPHS • TEST STRATEGI

SRA Skills Handbook
Using Science

Teach Cross-Curricular Skills to Students

The "How To" Format Helps You Teach Students Efficiently and Effectively

The **Skills Handbook** Using Science program integrates skills and content, which maximizes precious classroom time without interfering with your core curriculum. It utilizes science content to teach valuable cross-curricular skills in a step-by-step format.

Each grade level contains skill lessons that are integrated with grade-specific science content. Students use science content as they develop and practice skills from across the curriculum (such as reading, writing, language arts, math, and science investigation skills). The books are organized into skill categories to help you identify what you want to teach in a quick and thorough manner.

Each book (Grades 3–6) also contains specific Test-Taking Strategies designed to help students develop techniques for analyzing and answering test questions.

▶ Select the skills you need.

▶ Teach the skills in any order.

▶ Work in small groups or as a whole class.

Students Learn to Master a Variety of Different Skills and Strategies, Including:

Investigating Skills, such as:
- How to Make a Hypothesis
- How to Control Variables
- How to Choose the Right Tool
- How to Design an Experiment

Reading and Thinking Skills, such as:
- How to Compare and Contrast
- How to Determine Cause and Effect
- How to Find the Main Idea
- How to Tell Fact from Opinion

Writing and Research Skills, such as:
- How to Write a Paragraph
- How to Write about a Process
- How to Write a Summary
- How to Use the Internet

Chart and Graph Skills, such as:
- How to Make a Line Graph
- How to Read a Circle Graph
- How to Make a Graphic Organizer
- How to Read a Time Line

Test-Taking Strategies, such as:
- Identifying Details
- Understanding Sequence
- Inferring
- Ignoring Irrelevant Information

• INVESTIGATING • READING • WRITING • CHARTS • GRAPHS • TEST STRATEGI

Using Science Content

Program Materials that Fit the Grade Level

STUDENT MATERIALS

Grades 1–2
Instructional Cards for each grade level (15-1/4" x 19-3/4")
- 16 full-color, two-sided cards
- Step-by-step skill instruction
- Highlighted vocabulary

Grades 3–6
Softcover **Student Edition** for each grade level
- Full-color
- Step-by-step skill instruction
- Highlighted vocabulary
- Skill Application
- Test-Taking Strategies

TEACHER MATERIALS

Grades 1–6
Softcover **Teacher Guide** for each grade level
- Learning objectives
- Correlations to National Science Standards
- Answers
- Options for additional activities and extensions
- Blackline Activity Masters for further skill development, practice, and enrichment (Grades 1–2)
- Reduced **Student Edition** pages (Grades 3–6) for reference
- Reduced **Instructional Cards** pages (Grades 1–2) for reference

SKILLS WORKBOOK

Grades 3–6
Consumable workbook for each grade level
- Additional skill practice
- Writing process reference

• INVESTIGATING • READING • WRITING • CHARTS • GRAPHS • TEST STRATEGI

Every Lesson Is Designed to Make

The Student Editions Are Carefully Structured to Guide Skill Development

1. Each lesson defines a skill and provides the content that will develop the skill.

2. Skill concepts are developed so they can be applied to a variety of situations.

3. Useful tips help students work with the skill.

Skill 31
HOW TO Do a Survey

Zzzzs in Good Health

When you were a baby, you probably slept about 16 hours a day. Now that you are in school, you can't do that! But getting enough sleep is important to your health.

Children your age should get between 9 and 12 hours of sleep every night. Your body needs sleep just like it needs food, exercise, and plenty of water. Getting enough sleep helps you feel calm. It also lets you think clearly. When you sleep, your body slows down and relaxes.

Sleep is so important that many scientists study it. One way to gather information about sleep habits is to talk to people. In a **survey,** you collect information from a group of people by asking them questions. A survey can have one or more questions. When you do a survey, you must keep track of how people answer.

STEPS IN Doing a Survey
Follow these steps to do a survey of your own.

1 Pick a Topic
Decide what type of information you want to collect. Do you want to know when people go to sleep or how many hours they sleep each night?

2 Write a Question
Write a question that asks what you want to know. Do not let your opinion affect the question. Don't ask questions that can be answered with just *yes* or *no.*

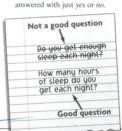

3 Make a Tally Sheet
Before you ask people the question, get organized. Write possible answers. You can group answers together to make recording easier.

Set up a tally sheet to keep track of the answers. Make a chart with the possible answers listed on the left. Leave room on the right to record.

Number of hours slept at night	Number of students
Less than 8 hours	
8 hours	
9 hours	
10 hours	
More than 10 hours	

152 / 153

STEPS IN Doing a Survey

4 Conduct the Survey
Now you are ready to ask people the question. Be polite and thank them when you are finished.

TIP Make sure your question asks for one piece of information at a time. This will make it easier to record the answers.

5 Record the Answers
As people answer your survey question, put tally marks, or short lines, next to the answers they give. Use one tally mark for each answer. When you reach five, draw the fifth tally mark across the others. This will make counting the tallies much easier later.

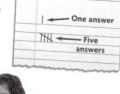

6 Count the Tallies
After you are finished doing the survey, count the tally marks by fives and ones. Add the number of fives and ones to get the total number of people who answered the same way. Write these numbers on your tally sheet in the correct answer rows.

7 Show Results
Show the information you collected in an easy-to-understand way. You can use a list, chart, or graph to show the results. Don't forget to title and label your graph so people know what information it shows.

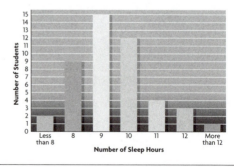

154 / 155

vi

• INVESTIGATING • READING • WRITING • CHARTS • GRAPHS • TEST STRATEGI

Learning Practical and Flexible

4. Examples provide skill application models.

5. Students practice and apply skills to new situations.

6. Test-taking tips guide students in testing situations.

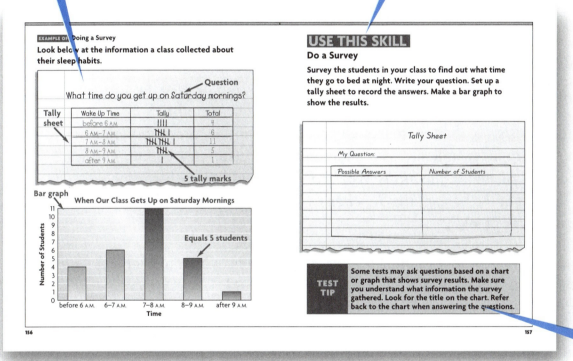

Student Edition, Grade 3

www.sra4kids.com

SRA
Skills Handbook
Using Science

The **Skills Handbook** *Using Science* program is a supplementary skills-based science program for grades 1 through 6. Each **Student Edition** is a resource guide that presents grade-specific science content while providing "how-to" instructions and opportunities for reinforcing important investigating, reading, thinking, writing, research, and math skills. In grades 3–6, test-taking tips and strategies are integrated throughout the skill lessons. The simplistic instructional design of the self-contained skill lessons in this program permits students to work independently with a minimum of teacher instruction. Further skill practice is offered in the **Skills Workbook** for grades 3–6. Blackline masters located at the back of the **Teacher's Guide** offer additional skill practice for grades 1 and 2.

Unlike other supplementary skill development programs, which restrict skill practice to specific curricular areas, the **Skills Handbook** *Using Science* program is a multicurricular resource. This makes the program a compelling skill supplement to any elementary reading, writing, math, or science program. In addition, if teachers do not use a traditional science series, the program provides them with the opportunity to touch on core science content that correlates to national standards in science.

SCIENCE STANDARDS

SKILL TITLE	CONTENT	SCIENCE STANDARDS
1 How to Make and Use a Model	Earthquakes	A: Abilities necessary to do scientific inquiry D: Changes in earth and sky
2 How to Measure	Temperature	A: Abilities necessary to do scientific inquiry B: Properties of objects and materials
3 How to Choose the Right Tool	Making a compost pile	A: Abilities necessary to do scientific inquiry C: Organisms and environments
4 How to Make a Hypothesis	Magnets	A: Abilities necessary to do scientific inquiry B: Light, heat, electricity, and magnetism
5 How to Collect Data	Reaction time	A: Abilities necessary to do scientific inquiry; Understanding about scientific inquiry
6 How to Control Variables	Changing how plants grow	A: Abilities necessary to do scientific inquiry C: The characteristics of organisms
7 How to Design an Experiment	What seeds need to germinate	A: Abilities necessary to do scientific inquiry C: The characteristics of organisms; Life cycles of organisms
8 How to Draw Conclusions	Dr. Eugenie Clark's shark experiments	A: Abilities necessary to do scientific inquiry C: The characteristics of organisms
9 How to Prepare an Observation Report	Observing mold on bread	A: Understanding about scientific inquiry C: Organisms and environments
10 How to Classify	Simple machines	B: Position and motion of objects
11 How to Compare and Contrast	The inner and outer planets	D: Objects in the sky
12 How to Determine Cause and Effect	Causes and effects of fire	B: Light, heat, electricity, and magnetism F: Personal health
13 How to Tell Fact from Opinion	Coral reefs	C: The characteristics of organisms; Organisms and environments
14 How to Find the Main Idea	Decomposers	C: Life cycles of organisms; Organisms and environments

SKILL TITLE	CONTENT	SCIENCE STANDARDS
15 How to Take Notes	Alternative fuel-powered vehicles	B: Light, heat, electricity, and magnetism F: Types of resources
16 How to Estimate	Food serving sizes	F: Personal health
17 How to Predict	Erosion	D: Properties of earth materials; Changes in earth and sky
18 How to Infer	Poison ivy	C: Organisms and environments F: Personal health
19 How to Make a Decision	Choosing a science fair project	F: Personal health
20 How to Work in a Group	Making a terrarium	C: The characteristics of organisms; Organisms and environments
21 How to Make a Learning Log	Hydrothermal vents	C: The characteristics of organisms; Organisms and environments
22 How to Write a Paragraph	Problems in national parks	F: Changes in environments; Science and technology in local challenges
23 How to Write an Outline	Natural resources	D: Properties of earth materials F: Types of resources
24 How to Write a Summary	Microbiology	C: Organisms and environments
25 How to Write a Description	Hot springs at Yellowstone National Park	D: Properties of earth materials
26 How to Write a Comparison/Contrast	How prosthetic limbs have changed over time	E: Understanding about science and technology F: Personal health
27 How to Write about a Process	Glassblowing	B: Properties of objects and materials
28 How to Use the Library	Volcanoes	D: Properties of earth materials; Changes in earth and sky
29 How to Write a Report	How bicycles have changed over time	E: Understanding about science and technology F: Personal health

SKILL TITLE	CONTENT	SCIENCE STANDARDS
30 How to Prepare a Display	Telescopes	A: Understanding about scientific inquiry B: Light, heat, electricity, and magnetism
31 How to Do a Survey	Cleaning up the environment	D: Properties of earth materials; Changes in earth and sky
32 How to Read a Time Line	The history of rockets	E: Understanding about science and technology G: Science as a human endeavor
33 How to Make a Table	Endangered species	C: Organisms and environments
34 How to Read a Bar Graph	Health effects of using tobacco	F: Personal health
35 How to Make a Line Graph	Tracking air temperature	D: Changes in earth and sky
36 How to Read a Circle Graph	Water conservation	F: Types of resources; Changes in environments
37 How to Make a Diagram	Insects	C: The characteristics of organisms; Life cycles of organisms
38 How to Read a Flowchart	How storms form	D: Changes in earth and sky
39 How to Make a Graphic Organizer	Lewis H. Latimer and the lightbulb	A: Understanding about scientific inquiry B: Light, heat, electricity, and magnetism
40 How to Read a Map	The Everglades	C: Organisms and environments F: Changes in environments

GRADE 4 SCOPE AND SEQUENCE

SKILLS	CONCEPTS DEVELOPED
1 How to Make and Use a Model	Three-dimensional model of a process
2 How to Measure	Use a thermometer to measure temperature, Celsius temperature scale
3 How to Choose the Right Tool	Choose between linear measurement tools
4 How to Make a Hypothesis	Use observations, prior knowledge, and questions to make a hypothesis
5 How to Collect Data	Collect and organize data in a table
6 How to Control Variables	Identify variables that are controlled and changed during an experiment
7 How to Design an Experiment	Write a step-by-step plan and list materials for an experiment
8 How to Draw Conclusions	Write a conclusion statement about the results of an experiment
9 How to Prepare an Observation Report	Write an observation report using the correct format
10 How to Classify	Classify objects by one or more attributes
11 How to Compare and Contrast	Use a T-chart to compare and contrast, signal words
12 How to Determine Cause and Effect	Use clue words, realize that often an effect is written first followed by its cause
13 How to Tell Fact from Opinion	Compare factual information with writing that contains opinions, use clue words to tell facts from opinions
14 How to Find the Main Idea	Identify the topic, topic sentence, detail sentences, and main idea in a passage
15 How to Take Notes	Concept webs, index cards, gathering grids, recording source information, using quotes
16 How to Estimate	Use concrete objects to estimate size
17 How to Predict	Use pictures to predict
18 How to Infer	Use observations and prior knowledge to make inferences
19 How to Make a Decision	Compare multiple choices, use a comparison chart to make a decision
20 How to Work in a Group	Establish a goal, choose tasks, make a schedule

SKILLS	CONCEPTS DEVELOPED
21 How to Make a Learning Log	Record responses to a reading passage
22 How to Write a Paragraph	Write a persuasive paragraph, topic sentence, supporting sentences, conclusion
23 How to Write an Outline	Topic outline, main ideas and details
24 How to Write a Summary	Differentiate between main ideas, details, examples, and reasons
25 How to Write a Description	Use descriptive language, adjectives, nouns, verbs, and adverbs
26 How to Write a Comparison/Contrast	Point-by-point comparison/contrast, use a T-chart, signal words, adjectives
27 How to Write about a Process	Explain the steps in a process, use lists
28 How to Use the Library	Use a card catalog to search for sources, use call numbers to locate sources in a library
29 How to Write a Report	Use index cards, organize information, create a bibliography
30 How to Prepare a Display	Make a three-sided display for experiments, models, and library research projects
31 How to Do a Survey	Word questions for a survey, tally results, show results graphically
32 How to Read a Time Line	Read horizontal time lines, understand different ways scales are represented
33 How to Make a Table	Define title, column, row
34 How to Read a Bar Graph	Read a vertical bar graph
35 How to Make a Line Graph	Draw and label a line graph to show how something changes over time
36 How to Read a Circle Graph	Read a circle graph to compare information
37 How to Make a Diagram	Picture diagram, Venn diagram, line diagram, cycle diagram
38 How to Read a Flowchart	Read a flowchart to follow steps in a process
39 How to Make a Graphic Organizer	5Ws and H chart, concept web, flowchart
40 How to Read a Map	Map title, legend, compass rose, scale

WRITING ASSESSMENT

SIX TRAITS OF WRITING

Good writing includes a variety of qualities or traits. By examining these traits individually, you can help a student better understand how to improve his or her work.

The traits of effective writing are as follows:

Ideas
Plenty of interesting information is given to hold the reader's attention. The ideas are used to help the reader make sense of a specific subject.

Organization
The writing should have a logical beginning, middle, and end. Main points are developed. An occasional surprise is inviting and not confusing.

Voice
This piece of writing should sound unique to the writer. This gives the writing personality and makes it seem like the writer is truly interested in the subject.

Word Choice
Words are specific and colorful. They add strong details to the writing and communicate the message well.

Sentence Fluency
The writing flows smoothly from one sentence to the next and from one paragraph to the next. It is almost as if there is a gentle rhythm to the writing when it is read aloud.

Grammar Conventions
Good writing will adhere to the basic conventions of the language. Grammar rules are followed with proper punctuation, spelling, and page layout.

These traits have been grouped under **Content**—what is said, **Style**—how it is said, and **Mechanics**—the polish. Use the three-point assessment rubric on page 1 to evaluate students' final drafts.

ASSESSMENT RUBRIC

Content Ideas and Organization

3 The writing task is completed in a lively and very well crafted manner. The writer uses a fresh, original approach to meet the guidelines.

2 The writing task is completed. All of the guidelines have been met in a very predictable way.

1 The writing is confusing to read or unfinished. It is difficult to find the different guidelines because of excess trivia or missing main points.

Specific content rubrics for each individual writing assignment can be found in the *Teacher's Guide*.

Style Voice, Word Choice, Sentence Fluency

3 Delightful word choices make the ideas crystal clear. The writer seems involved and brings the topic to life. The writing has a rhythm that is playful and easy to read aloud.

2 Words chosen are appropriate but sometimes simplistic or repetitive. Words are clear but lack "sparkle." The writer seems somewhat interested in the topic but a feeling of distance still remains. The writing sometimes runs on or feels choppy.

1 Words are often used incorrectly. Word choice is simplistic and may be muddled. The writer seems not to care about the topic. The writing contains many problems with sentence boundaries and is difficult to read.

Mechanics Grammar Conventions

3 No major errors. A few minor errors exist but they do not cause any reader confusion. Spelling, capitalization, punctuation, and usage are well done.

2 One major or some minor errors may cause reader confusion. Spelling, capitalization, punctuation, and usage are mostly correct.

1 Difficult to read. Many major and minor errors cause reader confusion. Repeated errors occur in spelling, capitalization, punctuation, and usage. Sentence boundaries may often be confused.

Skill 1
HOW TO
Make and Use a Model

Shaking in Your Shoes

At a Glance
Students will learn how to make and use a model by looking at models of an earthquake's causes and effects.

Objectives
- Realize that a model can help explain a process, a structure, or a relationship.
- Describe the steps in making and using a model.
- Identify similarities and differences between a model and a real process.
- Understand the causes of earthquakes.
- Infer the relationship between a model and an earthquake's cause and effect.

Reduced Student Pages
Teacher's Guide p. 100

Skills Workbook
For more practice making and using models, use **Skills Workbook** pages 1–2.

Correlation to Standards
Content Standard A: Abilities necessary to do scientific inquiry

Content Standard D: Changes in earth and sky

More About
Earthquakes
Many earthquakes occur along faults. Scientists classify faults into three groups. In a strike-slip fault, the rocks slide past each other without moving up or down. At a normal fault, the rocks on one side of the fault are higher than the rocks on the other side. When the rock layers move, one side slips down. A third type of fault is called a reverse fault. Movement can force the rocks on one side of a reverse fault to ride up and over the rocks on the other side.

Answers
Use This Skill, Student Edition p. 7
1. Earth
2. a building
3. By shaking the pan to move the water, you show how Earth's surface moves during an earthquake and how this movement can damage buildings and other structures.
4. The water moves in a similar way to the ground. The toothpick building can be damaged just like a real building.
5. The water's movement in the model is much gentler than Earth's movement in a real earthquake. The damage to real buildings could be much greater than the damage to the toothpick structure. Also, when real buildings collapse they can hurt people who are inside or nearby.

Activity
Have students use craft sticks or twigs to model how Earth's surface can move and break during an earthquake. Provide each student with goggles and a stick. Holding one end of the stick in each hand, students should slowly bend the stick, stopping just before it breaks. Tell students to repeat the activity, this time bending the stick as far as they can. After students are done with the activity, ask them to explain how the activity models what can happen to Earth's surface during an earthquake.

Outside Resources
Internet
Earthquake for Kids
earthquake.usgs.gov/4kids/

FEMA for Kids: Earthquakes
www.fema.gov/kids/quake.htm

Literature
Eyewitness: Volcano & Earthquake by Susanna Van Rose. DK Publishing, 2000.

If You Have Time…
Skill 1 Options

Research
Students may be interested in researching the question of whether animals can predict earthquakes and theories about how they do so. Suggest that students begin by searching the Internet for information on this topic. Remind students to carefully choose sources, because this is an area of speculation in the scientific community. Students may want to present their information in the form of a debate, with one side taking the position that animals can predict earthquakes and the other side presenting information or opinions to the contrary.

Did You Know?
American architect Frank Lloyd Wright designed the Imperial Hotel in Tokyo with the goal that the building be able to withstand the city's frequent earthquakes. Calling his design a "jointed monolith," Wright created a building composed of smaller independent parts with expansion joints between them. The entire structure floated on the site's underlying mud foundation. When a severe earthquake hit Tokyo on the morning of the hotel's official opening, September 1, 1923, the hotel suffered only modest damage.

Skill 2
HOW TO
Measure

Using a Thermometer

At a Glance
Students will learn how to measure the temperature of air and of liquids.

Objectives
- Name the scale that scientists use to measure temperature.
- Describe the steps in measuring temperature.
- Differentiate between correct and incorrect techniques for measuring temperature.

Reduced Student Pages
Teacher's Guide pp. 101–102

Skills Workbook
For more practice measuring, use **Skills Workbook** pages 3–4.

Correlation to Standards
Content Standard A: Abilities necessary to do scientific inquiry

Content Standard B: Properties of objects and materials

More About
Heat and Temperature
Scientists distinguish between heat and temperature. Heat is a form of energy, transferred from one substance to another as the result of a difference in temperature. Temperature is a measure of the amount of "heat" energy present in a substance. Because heat is a form of energy, it can be converted into work and measured. Scientists measure heat's work in units called calories and BTUs (British thermal units).

Answers
Use This Skill, Student Edition p. 13
The picture on the left shows the correct way to measure the temperature of a liquid. The picture on the right is wrong because it shows the thermometer touching the side and bottom of the beaker. When measuring the temperature of a liquid, you should hold the thermometer so that the bulb is in the middle of the liquid.

Activity

Provide an opportunity for students to practice measuring the temperature of air and liquids as they observe temperature changes. Before beginning this activity, fill a pitcher with water and allow it to reach room temperature. Have students measure and record the air temperature in the room. Then have students fill a small beaker with the room temperature water, a second beaker with ice water, and a third beaker with hot water. Have students measure the temperature of the water in each beaker and record their measurements. Every 15 minutes have the students measure and record the air and water temperatures until all four temperatures are the same.

Outside Resources
Literature

Hot and Cold by Rebecca M. Hunter. Raintree Steck-Vaughn Publishers, 2000.

How Do We Know How to Measure? by Victor Osborne. Raintree Steck-Vaughn Publishers, 1995.

Physics for Kids: 49 Easy Experiments with Heat by Robert W. Wood. Tab Books, 1990.

Science Projects about Temperature and Heat by Robert Gardner and Eric Kemer. Enslow Publishers, Inc., 1994.

If You Have Time...
Skill 2 Options

Research

Students may be interested in researching the history of the thermometer, focusing on the contributions of Galileo, Daniel Fahrenheit, Anders Celsius, and Lord Kelvin. Suggest that students use an encyclopedia, the Internet, or another resource to find information, and then share their findings in an annotated time line.

Skill Help

One of the most common errors in measuring temperature is failing to correctly calculate the value of each scale line on the thermometer. Help students get in the habit of always checking the thermometer scale before beginning to measure. Tell them to first look at the numbers marked on the thermometer and then count the number of lines between numbers to determine each line's value.

Skill 3
HOW TO
Choose the Right Tool

Making a Compost Pile

At a Glance
Students will learn how to choose the right tool by looking at the process of building a compost pile.

Objectives
- Understand the purpose of a tool.
- Explain the steps in choosing the right tool.
- Analyze the applications and advantages of specific linear measurement tools.
- Infer the reasons for choosing specific measuring tools when making a compost pile.
- Define *compost*.
- Choose the best linear measurement tool for different jobs.

Reduced Student Pages
Teacher's Guide pp. 102–103

Skills Workbook
For more practice choosing the right tool, use **Skills Workbook** pages 5–6.

Correlation to Standards
Content Standard A: Abilities necessary to do scientific inquiry

Content Standard C: Organisms and environments

More About
Composting
In a really good compost pile, yard waste breaks down in a matter of weeks. Providing microorganisms with just the right conditions speeds the process along. Plant materials contain carbon and nitrogen—two elements that microorganisms use as food. Microorganisms also need air and water to survive. Turning a compost pile regularly supplies sufficient air. In most cases rain provides adequate water. The more surface area the microorganisms have to work on, the faster the process goes. That is why experts recommend that people shred or chop twigs and other larger plant materials before adding them to the compost pile.

Answers
Use This Skill, Student Edition p. 17
1. ruler
2. tape measure
3. tape measure
4. ruler
5. ruler
6. meterstick
7. tape measure
8. meterstick
9. tape measure
10. ruler

Skill Help

Students may not understand that the reason for choosing a particular linear measurement tool has more to do with accuracy than with time saving and convenience. The problem with measuring a long distance with a ruler or meterstick instead of a tape measure lies in the error that can be introduced each time the device must be picked up and placed in position. Demonstrate this effect by having six groups of students measure the width of the classroom. Have two groups use rulers, two groups use metersticks, and two groups use tape measures. Compare the measures of each group, focusing students' attention on the reasons for the differences in each group's results.

Outside Resources

Internet

Build a Backyard Compost Pile
www.mastercomposter.com/pile/bldapile.html

Composting in Schools
www.cfe.cornell.edu/compost/schools.html

Worm Composting Basics
www.cfe.cornell.edu/compost/worms/wormhome.html

Literature

Compost Critters by Bianca Lavies. Dutton Children's Books, 1993.

Squirmy Wormy Composters by Bobbie D. Kalman and Janine Schaub. Crabtree Publishing Company, 1992.

If You Have Time...
Skill 3 Options

Activity

On index cards or strips of paper write descriptions for items or distances students should measure. Possible prompts include *distance from your desk to the board, height of your locker, width of the door, size of your science book,* and so on. Put all the cards in a box or bowl, and then have students take turns drawing a card and choosing the tool they would use to make the measurements. After each student has drawn one card, have students carry out the measurements described on their cards.

Research

Students may be interested in researching the topics of indoor composting and worm composting and investigating how to start a home or classroom composting project. Suggest that students find out how to build indoor compost and worm bins and learn what materials are necessary to get started. After students have completed their research, you might want to use the information they gathered to help you set up a classroom worm bin or other indoor composting project.

Skill 4
HOW TO
Make a Hypothesis

Magnet Mysteries

At a Glance
Students will learn how to make a hypothesis by looking at observations and questions about magnets.

Objectives
- Realize that a hypothesis is a statement that tries to answer a question about how or why something happens.
- Describe the steps in making a hypothesis.
- Infer the relationship between observations and questions about magnets and a hypothesis about how magnets work.
- Define *magnet*.
- Identify poorly-worded hypotheses and explain their weaknesses.

Reduced Student Pages
Teacher's Guide pp. 103–104

Skills Workbook
For more practice making a hypothesis, use *Skills Workbook* pages 7–8.

Correlation to Standards
Content Standard A: Abilities necessary to do scientific inquiry

Content Standard B: Light, heat, electricity, and magnetism

More About
Magnetic Force
A magnet is surrounded by a magnetic field—the area around the magnet in which magnetic forces can be observed. Magnetic forces cause attraction or repulsion, that is pushes or pulls, on other magnets and iron-containing materials. When a magnet attracts an iron-containing material, it magnetizes that material, making it into a temporary magnet. When the iron-containing material or object is removed from the magnetic field, the temporary magnet loses its magnetism. Some magnetic materials, such as an iron-containing rock called magnetite or lodestone, are found naturally in Earth.

Answers
Use This Skill, Student Edition p. 21
1. worded incorrectly; should be written in an *if . . . then* statement
2. worded incorrectly; should not be written as a question
3. worded incorrectly; should not be written as a question
4. worded correctly
5. worded incorrectly; should not be written as a question
6. worded incorrectly; should be written in an *if . . . then* statement
7. worded correctly
8. worded incorrectly; should not be written as a question

If You Have Time...
Skill 4 Options

Research
Students may be interested in researching the topic of electromagnets to learn how scientists use electric current to create electromagnets. Encourage students to find out how electromagnets are used in modern devices such as electric motors, televisions, maglev trains, computers, and telephones. Suggest that students present their information in a diagram or other visual format.

Skill Help
Some students may confuse a hypothesis with a conclusion. Explain that conclusions are based on the results of an activity, but a hypothesis is written before an activity begins. Thus, a hypothesis is a prediction, not an explanation. Discourage students from thinking that each hypothesis they write must always turn out to be correct.

Activity
Have students conduct an activity to observe what happens when a magnet comes into contact with a mixture of iron filings and sand. Explain the activity and direct students to write a hypothesis before they begin. Then have students wear goggles as they mix together equal amounts of iron filings and sand in a plastic dish. Have students stir the sand and iron filings until they are completely mixed together. Tell students to bring a magnet close to the dish, observing what happens to the mixture. Have students repeat the test, then compare their results to the hypothesis they wrote before starting the activity.

Did You Know?
A bar magnet has a north pole and a south pole. If you break the bar magnet in half, the resulting halves will each have a north pole and a south pole. If you break the halves in half again, each piece will still have a north pole and a south pole. No matter how many times you break the bar or how small the pieces, each segment will end up with a north pole and a south pole.

Skill 5
HOW TO Collect Data

Think Fast!

At a Glance
Students will learn how to collect data by looking at measurements and statistics collected for reaction times.

Objectives
- Realize that scientists collect data from many trials in order to draw meaningful conclusions.
- Describe the steps in collecting data.
- Examine data about reaction times and the process used to collect it.
- Define *reaction time.*
- Display data in a table.

Reduced Student Pages
Teacher's Guide pp. 104–105

Skills Workbook
For more practice collecting data, use *Skills Workbook* pages 9–10.

Correlation to Standards
Content Standard A: Abilities necessary to do scientific inquiry

Content Standard A: Understanding about scientific inquiry

More About
Fast Reactions
Blinking and sneezing are reflex actions. Each reflex involves a stimulus that causes an automatic response. Scientists call these reactions unconditioned reflexes, and they take place regardless of past experiences or teaching. Conditioned reflexes are another kind of reflex action. They work by associating an automatic reaction with a particular stimulus, such as when a dog's mouth waters in response to the smell of food. Other reactions, such as swinging a bat, may appear automatic. In reality they are complex skills called psychomotor or perceptual-motor skills. Reaction time for these skills can be affected by a variety of factors, including intensity of the stimuli, prior experience, practice, environmental factors, mood, and so on.

Answers
Use This Skill, Student Edition p. 27
Students should display the data in a table.

1. time measurements; data about reaction times
2. seconds

Research
Students may be interested in researching the topic of reflex actions and conditioned reflexes to learn the difference between these acts and voluntary reactions. Suggest that students give demonstrations or draw pictures to illustrate reflex actions, such as blinking, the knee jerk response, and the startle response, and some voluntary reactions, such as catching a falling object.

Did You Know?
Lack of practice isn't the only factor that adversely affects reaction time. Lack of oxygen, especially as a result of high altitudes, slows the body's reaction time. Age also impacts performance. For simple hand or foot reactions, peak skills are attained between ages 15 and 20. After that, the body begins a slow, gradual decline.

If You Have Time…
Skill 5 Options

Activity
Have students conduct the activity shown on **Student Edition** page 27. Suggest that students begin by making a table where they can record their data. Then have students conduct five trials before stopping to compare their data with those shown on the **Student Edition** page 27. Have students conduct five more trials. Each day for one week have students repeat the activity. Then have students evaluate the data, looking for trends in their reaction times. Are their scores better on the last day than on the first?

Outside Resources
Internet
Online Reaction Time Activity: Hit-the-Dot
faculty.washington.edu/chudler/java/dottime.html

The Reflex Tester
www.happyhub.com/network/reflex/

Science of Baseball
netra.exploratorium.edu/baseball/index.html

Skill 6
HOW TO
Control Variables

Changing How Plants Grow

At a Glance
Students will learn how to control variables by looking at factors that affect plant growth.

Objectives
- Realize that scientists control variables in a scientific investigation in order to draw meaningful conclusions.
- Describe the steps in controlling variables.
- Examine the impact of changing a variable in an experiment about plant growth.
- Understand what plants need to grow.
- Identify variables in an experiment about plant growth.

Reduced Student Pages
Teacher's Guide p. 106

Skills Workbook
For more practice controlling variables, use *Skills Workbook* pages 11–12.

Correlation to Standards
Content Standard A: Abilities necessary to do scientific inquiry

Content Standard C: The characteristics of organisms

More About
The Study of Plants
Botanists study the structure and form of plants, the functions of plant structures, and the interactions between plants and the environment. Botany also deals with the classification, identification, and naming of plants. Plants are extremely sensitive to their environments. Conditions such as climate and soil largely determine where and how plants grow.

Answers
Use This Skill, Student Edition p. 31
The variable is the size of the pot.
She hopes to answer the question, Does the size of the pot affect plant growth?

Students should provide at least three other variables and questions. Possible variables and questions are given below.

Water: Does the amount of water affect the plants' growth?
Time when watered: Does the time of day plants are watered affect the plants' growth?
Soil: Does the type of soil affect the plants' growth?
Light: Does the amount of light affect the plants' growth?
Temperature: Does temperature affect the plants' growth?
Material of pot: Does the material from which the pot is made affect the plants' growth?
Fertilizer: Does fertilizer affect the plants' growth?

Skill Help
Some students may have trouble identifying variables that can change in an experiment. To help students more easily identify variables, tell them to list all the choices they must make in an experiment. For instance, in an experiment growing seeds, the investigator chooses the type of seed, where to plant the seeds, how deeply to plant the seeds, the substance in which the seeds are planted, the amount of water to give to the seeds, the place where the planted seeds are left to grow, and so on. Each of these choices deals with a variable that can be changed or held constant in an experiment.

Outside Resources
Internet
The Great Plant Escape
www.urbanext.uiuc.edu/gpe/

Why Do Plants Have Flowers?
www.cnps.org/kidstuff/pollin.htm

Literature
How Plants Grow by Malcolm Penny. Benchmark Books, 1997.

Janice VanCleave's Plants: Mind-Boggling Experiments You Can Turn into Science Fair Projects by Janice Pratt VanCleave. John Wiley & Sons, 1997.

3D Eyewitness: Plant by John Akeroyd. DK Publishing, 1998.

If You Have Time...
Skill 6 Options

Did You Know?
In 1753 Swedish botanist Carl Linnaeus established the practice of naming plants by genus and species, a practice still in use today. The genus is the generic name that includes closely related species. A species is defined in part by external similarities and, in applicable species, the organisms' ability to interbreed.

Research
Students may be interested in focusing their research on plants that live in a particular vegetative region, such as a desert, rain forest, tropical savannah, deciduous forest, Arctic tundra, or taiga. Suggest that students work in groups, with each group reporting on a different region. Have students create displays with maps showing the location they studied, a description of the climate and soil conditions there, and facts about the plants that thrive in that part of the world.

Skill 7
HOW TO
Design an Experiment

What Do Seeds Need?

At a Glance
Students will learn how to design an experiment by reading about an experiment with seeds.

Objectives
- Realize that scientists design an experiment to gain information and test a hypothesis.
- Describe the steps in designing an experiment.
- Analyze the connections between a hypothesis about seeds and an experiment designed to test the hypothesis.
- Explain how seeds germinate.
- Design an experiment to test the effect of light on seeds.

Reduced Student Pages
Teacher's Guide pp. 107–108

Skills Workbook
For more practice designing an experiment, use **Skills Workbook** pages 13–14.

Correlation to Standards
Content Standard A: Abilities necessary to do scientific inquiry

Content Standard C: The characteristics of organisms

Content Standard C: Life cycles of organisms

More About
Seeds
A radish is a flowering plant. Seeds from flowering plants consist of the immature plant, called the embryo, a supply of stored food, called the endosperm, and a seed coat, or protective outer coating. Seeds need water, oxygen, and the proper temperature and light conditions in order to germinate. When a seed germinates, it takes in water and oxygen through its seed coat. The embryo begins to get energy from the endosperm. A small root, called the radicle, grows down from the embryo. A shoot, called the plumule, grows up toward light and air. Then seed leaves, called the cotyledons, begin to form.

Answers
Use This Skill, Student Edition p. 37
Students' experiments will vary. Students' experiments should test the hypothesis: If groups of seeds receive different amounts of light, then more seeds will germinate in the group with the most light. They should change the amount of light seeds receive but keep other variables in the experiment constant. They should list the steps they would follow and the materials they would use.

If You Have Time...
Skill 7 Options

Skill Link
Controlling variables is an essential element of any well-designed experiment. For further help controlling variables and more experiments with plants, see **Skill 6: How to Control Variables** on *Student Edition* pages 28–31.

Research
Students may be interested in focusing their research on how humans use seeds and in what fruits certain seeds are found. Rice, soybeans, peanuts, beans, and corn are seeds, all of which are important food sources for much of the world. Have students choose one or more favorite foods and find out what plants and plant parts go into the food.

Outside Resources
Literature
Eyewitness: Plant by David Burnie, Paul Burne, Karl Shone, and Andrew McRobb. DK Publishing, 2000.

The Life of Plants by M. Angels Julivert. Chelsea House, 1994.

Looking at Plants by David Suzuki and Barbara Hehner. John Wiley & Sons, 1992.

Skill Help
Some students may have trouble writing an experimental procedure in sequential order. Suggest that students start by visualizing the experiment, concentrating on each step they will take. Then have them write what they visualized, putting each step on a separate index card or strip of paper. Tell students to number the cards to show the step-by-step order. Encourage students to reorder the cards if they need to improve the sequence of steps before they write the final plan on separate paper.

Discussion
Ask students why it is important to write the hypothesis, plan, and list of materials before beginning an experiment. Remind them that scientists often conduct many trials of an experiment before drawing conclusions. Following the exact same procedure and using the same materials is one way that scientists control variables.

Skill 8
HOW TO
Draw Conclusions

Eugenie Clark Studies Sharks

At a Glance
Students will learn how to draw conclusions as they read about Dr. Eugenie Clark's experiments with sharks.

Objectives
- Realize that scientists draw conclusions to explain the results of experiments.
- Describe the steps in drawing conclusions.
- Infer the relationship between conclusions and the observations that support them.
- Read about the experiments of Dr. Eugenie Clark.
- Draw conclusions from an experiment on shark behavior.

Reduced Student Pages
Teacher's Guide pp. 108–109

Skills Workbook
For more practice drawing conclusions, use *Skills Workbook* pages 15–16.

Correlation to Standards
Content Standard A: Abilities necessary to do scientific inquiry

Content Standard C: The characteristics of organisms

More About
Sharks
Fossil evidence shows that sharks existed about 400 million years ago, making them among Earth's oldest living creatures. Today scientists group sharks into eight orders that contain about 370 known species. Large sharks are at the top of the ocean food chain. The shark's ability to detect sounds from a distance, along with its keen sense of smell, sensitivity to nearby movement, and ability to see in dim light, make it a highly efficient predator.

Answers
Use This Skill, Student Edition p. 41
The results show that in order to get food the shark changed its habit of swimming to the right. The results support the hypothesis.

Did You Know?
The shark's skin is rough and covered with scales that look like small shark teeth. Scientists theorize that sharks' teeth evolved from modifications to these scales.

Skill Help
Some students may have trouble distinguishing between drawing conclusions and writing a summary. Emphasize that conclusions explain the meaning behind the observations and results. In contrast, a summary retells the process and restates the observations without reflecting on the meaning or implications.

Activity
If an appropriate class pet is available, have students design a plan for teaching the pet a new behavior. Have students write a hypothesis, carry out the experiment, and draw conclusions from their observations. Alternatively, have students make observations about other animals in the home, such as a family pet. Have students draw conclusions based on these observations. Remind students to begin by making a hypothesis.

If You Have Time…
Skill 8 Options

Outside Resources
Internet
National Aquarium in Baltimore: Sharks
www.aqua.org/animals/species/sharks.html

Literature
Fish Watching with Eugenie Clark by Michael Elsohn Ross. Carolrhoda Books, 2000.

Shark Lady by Ann McGovern. Demco Media, 1994.

Discussion
After students finish reading the lesson, ask them to explain the impact of Eugenie Clark's conclusions about sharks. Ask students to think of other scientific conclusions that have greatly impacted the thinking or behavior of the public. Suggest that students might want to consider the results of medical research and the conclusions doctors have reached about the causes of serious illnesses, such as heart disease and lung cancer, as they answer this question.

Skill 9
HOW TO
Prepare an Observation Report

Curious about Mold

At a Glance
Students will learn how to prepare an observation report by looking at an investigation with bread mold.

Objectives
- Realize that an observation report provides a written summary of a scientific investigation.
- Explain the steps in preparing an observation report.
- Describe the purpose, procedure, and observations from an experiment with mold.
- Summarize the results of an experiment with mold.
- Understand the characteristics of mold.
- Write an observation report.

Reduced Student Pages
Teacher's Guide pp. 109–110

Skills Workbook
For more practice preparing an observation report, use *Skills Workbook* pages 17–18.

Correlation to Standards
Content Standard A: Understandings about scientific inquiry

Content Standard C: Organisms and their environments

More About
Mold
Fungi such as molds obtain food by releasing enzymes into organic matter. From outside the mold's body, the enzymes digest the food, which the mold then absorbs. Enzymes work faster as the temperature rises (as long as it doesn't get too hot). That is why mold develops more quickly on bread kept at room temperature than on bread stored in a refrigerator. The optimal temperature for mold growth is about 27 °C.

Answers
Use This Skill, Student Edition p. 47
Students' observation reports will vary but should include the following: a statement of purpose, an explanation of the procedure, a summary of observations, and a conclusion that the investigation supports. Students' observation reports should be based on the information provided on *Student Edition* page 47.

Skill Link
Drawing conclusions is an important skill when writing an observation report. For further help drawing conclusions, see **Skill 8: How to Draw Conclusions** on *Student Edition* pages 38–41.

Did You Know?
Penicillin comes from the *Penicillium* mold. The name *Penicillium* comes from the Latin word *penicillus,* meaning "brush." When viewed with a microscope, the bluish-green *Penicillium* mold has a brushlike appearance.

Discussion
Ask students how they could use an observation report about an experiment. Guide them in understanding that they could share it with another student who might want to conduct the same experiment, read it as a guide for their own repeat tests, or use it as a springboard from which to develop new questions and hypotheses for future experiments.

If You Have Time...
Skill 9 Options

Outside Resources
Internet
Fun Facts about Fungi
www.herb.lsa.umich.edu/kidpage/factindx.htm

The Microbial World: Penicillin and other antibiotics
helios.bto.ed.ac.uk/bto/microbes/penicill.htm

Natural Perspective: Fungus Kingdom
www.perspective.com/nature/fungi

Literature
Slime Molds and Fungi by Elaine Pascoe. Blackbirch Marketing, 1998.

Skill Help
Some students may have a hard time determining the amount of detail to include in an observation report. Remind them that an observation report should summarize the purpose, procedure, observations, and conclusions. Although the information should be complete, the report should be brief and to the point. Students need not provide an extensive materials list or a finely detailed explanation of the procedure.

Skill 10
HOW TO
Classify

Machines Make Work Easier

At a Glance
Students will learn how to classify objects by reading about simple machines.

Objectives
- Define *classify*.
- Examine examples of classification.
- Identify characteristics of simple machines.
- Classify simple machines based on features they share.

Reduced Student Pages
Teacher's Guide p. 111

Skills Workbook
For more practice classifying, use **Skills Workbook** pages 19–20.

Correlation to Standards
Content Standard B: Position and motion of objects

More About
Levers
Levers are simple machines that can be divided into three classes. With a first-class lever, the fulcrum (a fixed pivot point) is located between the effort and the resistance forces. A seesaw is a first-class lever. Someone pushes down (the effort) to lift someone else up (the resistance or load). With a second-class lever, the resistance is between the effort and the fulcrum. A wheelbarrow or bottle opener is a second-class lever. With a third-class lever, the effort is between the resistance and the fulcrum. Tweezers and tongs are third-class levers.

Answers
Use this Skill, Student Edition p. 53
Students should sort objects into two groups. Group names should be *wheel and axle* and *wedge*. Items in the wheel and axle group: bicycle pedal, pencil sharpener, and doorknob. Items in the wedge group: doorstop, saw, and ax.

Skill Help

If students have difficulty classifying objects, divide the class into small groups. Give each group a "mystery box" with six to ten common household or school items that could be classified in different ways. Have students classify the items based on common features and have them write group names.

Skill Link

Tables and graphic organizers are useful ways to classify information. To help students with these skills, see **Skill 33: How to Make a Table** on *Student Edition* pages 166–169 and **Skill 39: How to Make a Graphic Organizer** on *Student Edition* pages 194–197.

Outside Resources

Literature

How Do You Lift a Lion? by Robert E. Wells. Albert Whitman & Co., 1996.

Machines: Mind-boggling Experiments You Can Turn Into Science Fair Projects by Janice VanCleave. John Wiley & Sons, Inc., 1993.

Simple Machines (Starting with Science) by Deborah Hodge. Kids Can Press, 2000.

Internet

Inventor's Toolbox: The Elements of Machines
www.mos.org/sln/Leonardo/InventorsToolbox.html

The Official Rube Goldberg Web Site
www.rube-goldberg.com

If You Have Time...
Skill 10 Options

Activity

- Have a scavenger hunt for simple machines. Student groups can look for two examples of each of the six simple machines in the classroom or bring examples from home.

- Have students cut out pictures of fruits and vegetables from magazines. Ask students to think of ways to classify the food, such as color, shape, taste, size, and type. See how many ways the food items can be grouped.

Research

- Have interested students research the simple machines that scholars think were used to build the pyramids in Egypt.

- Interested students may want to research Rube Goldberg, a cartoonist who drew complicated machines that could be used to accomplish simple tasks. Students can look for illustrations of the machines Goldberg drew and try to draw their own inventions.

Skill 11
HOW TO
Compare and Contrast

Comparing the Planets

At a Glance
Students will learn how to compare and contrast by reading about the planets.

Objectives
- Follow steps to compare and contrast.
- Recognize signal words for comparing and contrasting when reading.
- Know similarities and differences between the inner and outer planets, and between Venus and Earth.
- Make a chart to compare and contrast Mars and Earth.

Reduced Student Pages
Teacher's Guide p. 112

Skills Workbook
For more practice comparing and contrasting, use **Skills Workbook** pages 21–22.

Correlation to Standards
Content Standard D: Objects in the sky

More About
Mars
Mars's surface is rocky, but the rocks are covered with a rusty dust. Because its axis is tilted, Mars has seasons, just as Earth does. During the windy season, wind storms blow the dust around. When the reddish dust is blown off the rocks in some areas, that part of the planet appears darker as it is viewed from Earth. Mars has two small moons, both covered with craters. Many U.S. spacecraft have visited Mars. Photographs show that Mars has many volcanoes, but astronomers do not think they are active. There is no evidence of water on the planet, but some scientists think there was water on Mars millions of years ago. In 1997, *Mars Global Surveyor* began to orbit Mars to map and photograph the planet's surface in detail.

Answers
Use This Skill, Student Edition p. 57
Students should make a chart showing how Mars and Earth are alike and different.
Similarities between the planets include: both are made of rocks and days on the planets are about the same length.
Differences between the planets include: Earth has green vegetation whereas Mars has reddish rocks; There is no life (as we know it) on Mars; There is only frozen water on Mars; Mars has no lakes or oceans; Mars's atmosphere is mostly carbon dioxide, and Earth's is mostly nitrogen and oxygen; Mars is half the size of Earth; One year on Mars equals two years on Earth; Mars has two moons, unlike Earth which has one moon.

Skill Link
For further help with comparing and contrasting, refer students to **Skill 26: How to Write a Comparison/Contrast** on *Student Edition* pages 126–131 and **Skill 37: How to Make a Diagram** on *Student Edition* pages 184–189.

Outside Resources
Literature
The Planets by Gail Gibbons. Holiday House, 1994.
Our Solar System by Seymour Simon. Morrow, 1992.

Internet
NASA Kids
kids.msfc.nasa.gov/
Your Weight on Other Worlds
www.exploratorium.edu/ronh/weight/

Skill Help
Students who struggle to compare and contrast using a chart may benefit from making Venn diagrams. Students should try using different kinds of organizers and choose the approach that seems to work best.

If You Have Time...
Skill 11 Options

Research
Interested students can choose two planets to research. Have them compare and contrast the two planets.

Did You Know?
Venus rotates so slowly that there are only two sunrises and sunsets each year on the planet.

Skill 12
HOW TO
Determine Cause and Effect

Fire!

At a Glance
Students will learn how to determine cause and effect by reading about the causes and effects of fire.

Objectives
- Define *cause* and *effect*.
- Recognize clue words to identify cause and effect.
- Realize that causes precede effects in real time.
- Identify cause-and-effect relationships in readings about fire.

Reduced Student Pages
Teacher's Guide p. 113

Skills Workbook
For more practice determining cause and effect, use **Skills Workbook** pages 23–24.

Correlation to Standards
Content Standard B: Light, heat, electricity, and magnetism

Content Standard F: Personal health

More About
Cooking Fires
To avoid starting a fire while cooking, follow these tips. Never leave food cooking on the stovetop or in the oven unattended. Keep cooking areas free of items that might catch on fire such as potholders, towels, curtains, and paper packaging. Turn pot handles inward so they can't be bumped or grabbed accidentally. Wear close-fitting clothes or sleeves rolled up when near open flames. Always keep a lid handy to smother grease fires. If a fire starts in your oven, turn off the heat and keep the door closed to keep flames from burning you or your clothes.

Answers
Use this Skill, Student Edition p. 61
Students should list at least three causes and effects. Possible cause and effect relationships include: **effect:** Many home fires **cause:** (are) caused by people who become careless while cooking; **effect:** stopping home fires **cause:** remove one or more parts of the fire triangle; **cause:** baking soda mixes with liquids in burning foods **effect:** carbon dioxide forms; **effect:** The (grease) fire goes out **cause:** because carbon dioxide keeps oxygen from reaching the fuel or burning food; **cause:** Putting a lid on a burning pot **effect:** smothers a fire; **effect:** A paper fire may stop **cause:** because water thrown on it smothers the fire; **cause:** Water thrown on a grease or electrical fire **effect:** will make these fires worse

Skill Help
To give students additional practice determining cause and effect, have students write sentences about events. Students can trade sentences with a partner and identify the cause and effect in each sentence.

Research
Have students who are interested in how fires affect their community contact the local fire department to get facts about the causes and effects of common fires in their neighborhoods. Have them gather information on fire safety and prevention.

Outside Resources
Literature
Catching Fire: The Story of Firefighting by Gene Kinton Gorrell. Tundra Books, 1999.

Fire Night! by Monica Driscoll Beatty and Christie Allan-Piper. Health Press, 1999.

Stop, Drop, and Roll (A book about fire safety) by Margery Cuyler. Simon and Schuster, 2001.

Internet
Smokey Bear
www.smokeybear.com

If You Have Time...
Skill 12 Options

Did You Know?
A fire that started nearly 40 years ago is still burning in an underground mine beneath Centralia, Pennsylvania. No one has figured out how to stop the flow of oxygen that keeps the fire burning.

Discussion
Discuss with students why it is important for them to know what causes fires and what to do if a fire starts in their homes. Have students talk about plans they have at school and at home for evacuating a burning building.

Skill 13
HOW TO
Tell Fact from Opinion

Coral Reefs

At a Glance
Students will learn how to distinguish facts from opinions as they read about coral reefs.

Objectives
- Recognize that both facts and opinions are used in writing.
- Differentiate facts from opinions.
- Understand how coral reefs form and why they are important.
- Identify facts and opinions in a reading passage about the effects of humans on coral reefs.

Reduced Student Pages
Teacher's Guide pp. 114–115

Skills Workbook
For more practice telling fact from opinion, use **Skills Workbook** pages 25–26.

Correlation to Standards
Content Standard C: The characteristics of organisms

Content Standard C: Organisms and environments

More About
Coral Reefs
A condition called bleaching is one factor affecting coral reefs. The affected corals expel the algae that live within their tissues, turn white, and eventually die if the bleaching continues. Scientists think that bleaching is caused by elevated ocean temperatures and other environmental stressors. The number of episodes of bleaching began increasing in the 1980s. The most extensive bleaching to date occurred in 1998. The death of the reefs would have a major economic and environmental impact.

Answers
Use This Skill, Student Edition p. 67
Answers will vary but should include one fact and one opinion.

Facts: When storms bury a reef under sand, the coral dies. Over the past 20 years, the water temperature has risen. If the water gets too warm, the corals die. Disease is killing the corals. The sea-fan coral in the Caribbean Sea is being killed by a type of fungus. Chemical pollution from herbicides and oil drilling has poisoned the water. Divers and boaters disturb and damage the reefs. If the reefs die, people will lose a main source of food.

Opinions: The damage being done to coral reefs around the world is terrible. Finding ways to protect the coral reefs should be one of the world's priorities.

If You Have Time...
Skill 13 Options

Did You Know?
The chalk that is used to write on chalkboards is made of calcium carbonate. This is the same chemical compound that makes up the skeletons of coral polyps.

Skill Help
To help students understand the difference between facts and opinions, have them write facts and opinions about their school in T-charts.

Research
Have students who are interested investigate the various ways coral reefs benefit people. Areas for investigation include: reef animals as a source of food and livelihood, coral reefs as protection from storms and coastal erosion, coral reefs as a source of new medicines, and the use of coral as replacement for bone in surgical procedures. Have students share their findings with the class.

Outside Resources
Literature
Dive to the Coral Reefs by Elizabeth Tayntor. Crown Publishers, Inc., 1986.

Life in the Coral Reef by Bobbie Kalman. Crabtree Publishers, 1996.

The Magic School Bus Takes a Dive by Joanna Cole. Scholastic, 1998.

Internet
Kingdom of Coral: Australia's Great Barrier Reef
www.nationalgeographic.com/ngm/0101/feature2/index.html

Coral Reef Protection
www.epa.gov/owow/oceans/coral/

Activity
- Have students use a world map to identify the locations of the coral reefs of the world. Some of these areas include the northwest coast of Africa, Madagascar, the northern coast of Australia, the Caribbean, the Philippines, Indonesia, southern India, and eastern China.
- Have students write news stories that contain facts about coral reefs. Then have students write editorials that contain opinions about coral reefs.

Skill 14
HOW TO
Find the Main Idea

Nature's Recyclers

At a Glance
Students will learn how to find the main idea of a passage as they read about decomposers.

Objectives
- Differentiate among topic sentences, main ideas, and detail sentences.
- Understand that the main idea of a paragraph is often in a topic sentence.
- Understand the role decomposers play in an ecosystem and identify examples of decomposers.
- Identify the main idea of a paragraph about bacteria.

Reduced Student Pages
Teacher's Guide pp. 115–116

Skills Workbook
For more practice finding the main idea, use *Skills Workbook* pages 27–28.

Correlation to Standards
Content Standard C: Life cycles of organisms

Content Standard C: Organisms and environments

More About
Decomposers in a Compost Pile
In a compost pile, decomposers work in many ways to break down organic material. Bacteria are the most numerous organisms in a compost pile. There are three basic types of bacteria and each is active within a specific temperature range, laying the foundation for the work of the next type. Other organisms that are larger than bacteria also play a role in turning organic material into compost. These organisms often feed on bacteria and their by-products. They include higher-form bacteria that live in the soil and provide nutrients for plants; fungi that break down organic material; and invertebrates such as mites, centipedes, sow bugs, beetles, wolf spiders, and redworms that chew and grind organic matter in the compost pile.

Answers
Use This Skill, Student Edition p. 71
Answers will vary but should include the main idea that some bacteria change dangerous chemicals into harmless ones.

Research
Interested students might want to read about mushroom farming. Students can also find out about the dangers of eating wild mushrooms.

Activity
Take students on a hike and look for examples of decomposers at work. Have students look for logs or tree stumps covered with lichens or mushrooms. Students can draw pictures of the decomposers they see.

Skill Link
Finding the main ideas of a passage is an important part of writing a summary. For more help with writing summaries, see **Skill 24: How to Write a Summary** on *Student Edition* pages 114–119.

If You Have Time...
Skill 14 Options

Did You Know?
Some insects and worms are decomposers. In one acre of land, more than a million earthworms can be found, eating an average of 10 tons of organic material and turning over about 40 tons of soil.

Outside Resources
Literature
The Magic School Bus Gets Eaten: A Book About Food Chains by Patricia Relf. Scholastic, 1996.

Scavengers and Decomposers: The Clean-up Crew by Pat Hughey. Simon and Schuster, 1984.

Skill 15
HOW TO
Take Notes

Alternative Fuel-Powered Vehicles

At a Glance
Students will learn how to take notes by reading about alternative fuel-powered vehicles.

Objectives
- Define *alternative fuel.*
- Recognize types of alternative fuels.
- Learn how to take notes from text.
- Take notes on a passage about hybrid electric vehicles.

Reduced Student Pages
Teacher's Guide pp. 116–117

Skills Workbook
For more practice taking notes, use **Skills Workbook** pages 29–30.

Correlation to Standards
Content Standard B: Light, heat, electricity, and magnetism

Content Standard F: Types of resources

More About
Biofuels: Alternative Fuels from Plants
Today the most widely used biofuel is bioethanol. Bioethanol is alcohol made from woody plants and agricultural and forestry residues that contain cellulose. Bioethanol is added to gasoline to improve vehicle performance and reduce air pollution. Another biofuel is biodiesel, which is made from vegetable oils, animal fats, and recycled greases. The oils or fats are combined with alcohol (such as ethanol) and then blended with conventional diesel fuel. U.S. producers of biodiesel use mostly recycled cooking oil and soy oil in their fuels.

Answers
Use this Skill, Student Edition p. 77
Students should write concise notes in a graphic organizer or on an index card. Notes should include the main ideas and supporting details and may include keywords, phrases, and abbreviations.

If You Have Time...
Skill 15 Options

Research
Have students find out more about the development of AFVs. Suggest they research when the first AFVs were introduced, current AFVs available for purchase, AFVs that may be added to the market in the future, and the advantages and disadvantages of owning an AFV.

Discussion
Have students discuss how people react when new technological ideas are introduced. Ask them how they think traditional car manufacturers felt about AFVs when they were first introduced. Ask them if they think everyone likes the idea of AFVs and to tell why or why not.

Skill Link
Taking notes requires the ability to organize information in a useful way. Refer students to **Skill 23: How to Write an Outline** on *Student Edition* pages 108–113 and **Skill 39: How to Make a Graphic Organizer** on *Student Edition* pages 194–197.

Did You Know?
During the summers of 1997 and 1998, Joseph Tickell used biodiesel in his small motor home he called the "Veggie Van." He drove around the United States educating people about alternative fuels. When he used recycled cooking oil from fast food restaurants, many people thought the exhaust smelled like french fries!

Skill Help
Students who have difficulty taking notes may benefit from experimenting with different note-taking styles. Some students may find using a concept web easier than other note-taking methods. Others may prefer a more structured note-taking approach such as outlining. Encourage students to find the note-taking style that works best for them and continue to use that approach.

Skill 16
HOW TO Estimate

One Serving, Please

At a Glance
Students will learn how to estimate serving sizes of foods as recommended by the Food Guide Pyramid.

Objectives
- Realize that estimating can be done by comparing objects to familiar concrete objects.
- Explain the steps in estimating.
- Interpret estimates for food servings.
- Estimate number of servings from each food group in personal daily diet.

Reduced Student Pages
Teacher's Guide p. 118

Skills Workbook
For help estimating, use *Skills Workbook* pages 31–32.

Correlation to Standards
Content Standard F: Personal health

More About
The Food Guide Pyramid
The Food Guide Pyramid was developed by the U.S. Department of Agriculture and contains five basic food groups. The foods in each group contain similar nutrients. Eating the recommended number of servings daily insures that one will get the nutrients needed to stay healthy. The Food Guide Pyramid is set up to visually represent how much of each kind of food one should eat daily. Serving size is important in controlling calorie intake.

The sixth group, fats, oils, and sweets, provides few valuable nutrients. Foods in this group should be eaten sparingly. For anyone older than five years old, no more than 30 percent of one's calorie intake should be from this food group.

Answers
Use This Skill, Student Edition p. 81
Students' food logs will vary. They should estimate and write how many servings from each food group they ate. Students' answers to the questions will vary but should reflect knowledge of serving sizes and suggested number of servings as given in the Food Guide Pyramid.

Research
Food pyramids for ethnic and special audiences are available. Have students research one of these pyramids to find out how they vary from the Food Guide Pyramid they have been studying.

Activity
Have students bring in boxes or packages from various foods. Have them determine how much of each item (for example, pieces of bread) is a serving size. Then have students calculate the greatest number or amount that would be needed to meet the recommended number of servings as specified by the Food Guide Pyramid.

Outside Resources
Literature
Food: Its Evolution Through the Ages by Piero Ventura. Houghton Mifflin Company, 1994.

Foodworks: Over 100 Science Activities and Fascinating Facts That Explore the Magic of Food from the Ontario Science Centre. Addison-Wesley Publishing Company, Inc., 1987.

Internet
Food and Nutrition Information Center
www.nalusda.gov/fnic/etext/000023.html#xtocid2381818

The Food Guide Pyramid
www.nalusda.gov:8001/py/pmap.htm

Dole 5 a Day
www.dole5aday.com

If You Have Time...
Skill 16 Options

Skill Help
Encourage students to determine their own concrete objects to help them estimate and remember what serving sizes of their favorite or most often eaten foods are. Have them measure actual food servings, determine objects that are about the same size, and list these in a chart or notebook for easy reference.

Did You Know?
Many restaurants serve larger portions than they did years ago. In the 1950s, a typical serving of French fries was about two ounces. Today a serving of French fries at most fast food restaurants is two or three times that size. A 1950s fast food hamburger was about one ounce. Today the typical hamburger is between four and ten ounces.

Skill 17
HOW TO Predict

Erosion

At a Glance
Students will learn how to make predictions by reading about erosion.

Objectives
- Define *predict*.
- Understand the steps in predicting.
- Observe from photos how erosion happens.
- Write a prediction about a rock formation shown in a photograph.

Reduced Student Pages
Teacher's Guide p. 119

Skills Workbook
For more practice predicting, use **Skills Workbook** pages 33–34.

Correlation to Standards
Content Standard D: Properties of earth materials

Content Standard D: Changes in earth and sky

More About
Erosion
Erosion is caused by gravity, glaciers, wind, running water, and waves. Gravity is a force that can pull rocks, dirt, or sand down a hill or cliff. Glaciers are large masses of slowly moving ice. As glaciers move downhill, they drag rocks and soil with them. Wind moves sand from place to place. It can also wear away a large rock, one particle at a time. Running water can move not only sand but big boulders as well. The faster a river flows, the more particles of sand and rock it can move. Waves along a shoreline carry sand from one beach to another. During storms, waves can pull whole cliffs out to sea, changing the shape of the coastline forever.

Answers
Use This Skill, Student Edition, p. 85
Students should predict that the base of the rock will eventually be completely worn away and that the rock will fall down.

If You Have Time...
Skill 17 Options

Skill Help
Some students may confuse making a prediction with guessing. Explain that, unlike guessing, a prediction is based on observations and what a person already knows or has experienced.

Research
Have students do research about the causes and effects of coastal erosion. Students can find out how people who live along coastlines cope with this problem.

Activity
Challenge students to find and photograph examples of erosion in your community. Then have them work together to create a display of their photographs, along with information cards that explain what is happening in each photo and predict what will happen in the future. If the site photographed presents a problem, students might also suggest a solution.

Did You Know?
Cape Hatteras Lighthouse in North Carolina's Outer Banks was moved in 1999 in order to preserve the lighthouse from the effects of coastal erosion. Years of erosion from storms and waves were causing the coastline to disappear, bringing the shore dangerously close to the lighthouse.

Outside Resources
Internet
Glacier
www.glacier.rice.edu/

Beach Erosion
whyfiles.org/091beach/

What Is a Mudslide?
www.disasterrelief.org/Disasters/971008landslide/

Skill 18
HOW TO
Infer

Leaves of Three, Let Them Be

At a Glance
Students will learn how to infer as they read about poison ivy and its effect on people and animals.

Objectives
- Explain the steps in inferring.
- Demonstrate an understanding of the importance of observation and previous knowledge to inferring.
- Make an inference about poison ivy's effect on wood rats.

Reduced Student Pages
Teacher's Guide p. 120

Skills Workbook
For more practice inferring, use **Skills Workbook** pages 35–36.

Correlation to Standards
Content Standard C: Organisms and environments

Content Standard F: Personal health

More About
Poison Ivy
All parts of poison ivy except the flowers contain an oil called urushiol. When this oil comes in contact with the skin, many people experience an allergic reaction. The oil can be transferred by brushing up against the plant, touching clothing or pets that have the oil on them, or coming in contact with smoke from burning the plants.

Answers
Use This Skill, Student Edition p. 89
1. The student saw a wood rat eating leaves from a vine. The student observed that the vine was poison ivy.
2. The student wondered how the rat could eat poison ivy.
3. The student knew that when he touched poison ivy, it gave him an itchy rash. He knew that his teacher said most animals were unaffected by the oil from poison ivy. He remembered that his teacher had said some animals eat poison ivy leaves and berries.
4. He combined what he saw with what he already knew. The information he already knew helped him explain what he observed.
5. He inferred that poison ivy oil must not affect wood rats.

Did You Know?
People should never assume that they are immune to the effects of the urushiol in poison ivy, poison oak, and poison sumac. It is possible to develop a sensitivity to urushiol after repeated exposures.

Activity
Have students find pictures of poison ivy and then make their own drawings of the plant. If possible, take students to a wooded area to search for and identify poison ivy. Be careful not to let students touch poison ivy.

Skill Help
To help students who are having difficulty understanding how to infer, provide additional situations in which the students may make inferences. Some situations are suggested here. Accept all logical answers.

- You hear a crash in the living room. When you go in, there is a ball on the couch next to a broken lamp.
- A girl in your class said she wasn't feeling well. Your teacher sent her to the school nurse, but she never came back.
- The dog is missing from your neighbor's yard. The neighbor's gate is open.

If You Have Time...
Skill 18 Options

Discussion
Ask students to give opinions on whether or not poison ivy should be eradicated. Encourage them to support their opinions.

Outside Resources
Literature
Let's Talk About Poison Ivy by Melanie Apel Gordon. The Rosen Publishing Group, Inc., 2000.

Internet
Outsmarting Poison Ivy and Its Cousins
www.fda.gov/fdac/features/796_ivy.html

The Secret of Silver Pond
www.nwf.org/rangerrick/2000/aug00/poisoni.html

Skill 19
HOW TO
Make a Decision

Choosing a Science Fair Project

At a Glance
Students will learn how to make a decision by reading about choosing a science fair project.

Objectives
- Define the steps in the decision-making process.
- Understand how to use personal goals to choose a science fair project.
- Use the steps in the decision-making process to choose a science fair project.

Reduced Student Pages
Teacher's Guide p. 121

Skills Workbook
For help making a decision, use **Skills Workbook** pages 37–38.

Correlation to Standards
Content Standard F: Personal health

More About
Science Fair Projects
Completing a science fair project involves a considerable amount of time to do properly. Success is not measured by the "rightness" or "wrongness" of students' findings but rather in the learning that takes place. Students should begin by choosing a topic that sparks their curiosity. To get topic ideas, students can look through science fair project books, search the Internet, brainstorm with friends, or ask parents and teachers for suggestions. Once a topic has been selected, students should develop a hypothesis and do a background research paper. Students should design and implement an experiment to test their hypothesis, copiously recording their observations and results along the way, because the next step is compiling the results and drawing conclusions. Finally, students must develop a neat, attractive display that summarizes the project.

Answers
Use This Skill, Student Edition p. 93
Answers will vary. Students should make a chart with advantages and disadvantages related to the proposed science projects on *Student Edition* page 93.

Outside Resources
Literature
The Chicken Doesn't Skate by Gordon Korman. Scholastic Inc., 1996.

The Complete Science Fair Handbook: For Teachers and Parents of Students In Grades 4–8 by Anthony Fredericks and Isaac Asimov. Goodyear Publishing Co., 1991.

Fifty Nifty Science Fair Projects by Carol Amato and Eric Ladizinsky. Lowell House Juvenile, 1993.

Internet
Internet Public Library Science Fair Project Resource Guide
www.ipl.org/youth/projectguide

Research
The International Science and Engineering Fair (ISEF) has delineated project categories. Have students research to find out what the categories are. Ask them to list between three and five that they had not known of or considered before. Then have them list two or three that interest them.

Activity
Ask students to make a list of science topics that interest them. Then have them think of advantages and disadvantages of each. If your school does not have a science fair, conduct one in your own classroom. Encourage students to develop and submit plans before beginning their projects.

If You Have Time...
Skill 19 Options

Discussion
Discuss with students the pros and cons (as they see them) of using animals in science fair experiments.

Skill Link
For further help in putting together science fair projects, refer to **Skill 29: How to Write a Report** on *Student Edition* pages 142–147 and **Skill 30: How to Prepare a Display** on *Student Edition* pages 148–153.

Skill 20
HOW TO
Work in a Group

Making a Terrarium

At a Glance
Students will learn how to work in a group by planning to make a terrarium.

Objectives
- Identify what it means to work in a group.
- Understand how to make a group plan.
- Analyze the tasks and the schedule needed to make a desert terrarium.
- Create a group plan for making a woodland terrarium.

Reduced Student Pages
Teacher's Guide p. 122

Skills Workbook
For more practice working in a group, use *Skills Workbook* pages 39–40.

Correlation to Standards
Content Standard C: The characteristics of organisms

Content Standard C: Organisms and environments

More About
Terrariums
There is very little care necessary after a terrarium is assembled. A terrarium should be placed in an area that is well lit but out of direct sunlight. When covered, a balanced terrarium provides excellent growing conditions because it preserves the temperature and moisture inside. If the terrarium clouds up with moisture, the lid can be opened to decrease the humidity. The addition of water is necessary only if condensation does not collect on the glass or plastic walls of the terrarium. If water is needed, it should be added a little at a time—one to two teaspoons per day until condensation appears.

Answers
Use This Skill, Student Edition p. 97
Answers will vary but should include the following: a goal statement/description of the project, a list of tasks that need to be done, each group member's job, the schedule of when jobs will be completed by each member, and the due date of the final project. Some students may include adjustments to the plan.

Did You Know?
Small animals such as salamanders, toads, lizards, snakes, and wood frogs can live in a woodland terrarium.

Outside Resources
Literature
Aquariums and Terrariums: A New True Book by Ray Broekel. Children's Press, 1982.

Terrarium Habitats by Kimi Hosoume and Jacqueline Barber. LHM Gems, 2000.

Internet
Build Your Own Terrarium
www.nationalgeographic.com/resources/ngo/education/plastics/buildframe.html

Skill Link
Knowing how to make decisions helps students successfully work in groups. For more information on this skill, refer students to **Skill 19: How to Make a Decision** on *Student Edition* pages 90–93.

If You Have Time...
Skill 20 Options

Activity
Have students work in groups to create desert or woodland terrariums. The students should research what plants and other materials to use and divide the tasks evenly among the group members.

Research
Have interested students interview a local florist for suggestions on the kinds of plants that do well in a woodland terrarium as well as additional information about making and maintaining a terrarium.

Skill 21
HOW TO
Make a Learning Log

Life at the Vents

At a Glance
Students will learn how to make a learning log as they read about hydrothermal vents.

Objectives
- Understand the structure and purpose of a learning log.
- Define *hydrothermal vents*.
- Describe life in the deep ocean.
- Write a learning log entry based on a reading passage.

Reduced Student Pages
Teacher's Guide p. 123

Skills Workbook
For more practice writing learning log entries, use **Skills Workbook** pages 41–42.

Correlation to Standards
Content Standard C: The characteristics of organisms

Content Standard C: Organisms and environments

More About
Zones in the Ocean
Scientists have divided the layers of the ocean into zones. Different organisms live in each of these zones because the organisms have adaptations that allow them to live in certain conditions. The *sunlit* zone is closest to the surface. Here the temperature of the water is affected by sunlight and seasonal changes. The *twilight* zone, which is below the sunlit zone, has very little light, colder temperatures, and more water pressure. There are no plants in this zone or the others below it because there is not enough light for plants to carry out photosynthesis. The *dark zone* is the next zone of the ocean. Here there is no light. The water pressure is intense and the water is very cold. Animals that live in this zone navigate by sound. The deepest part of the ocean is called the *abyss.* As in the dark zone, there is no light, water temperature is lower, and water pressure is higher. Less is known about the abyss than the other zones of the ocean. Hydrothermal vents are located in this zone.

Answers
Use This Skill, Student Edition p. 103
Students' learning logs will vary. They should write responses to the paragraph. Responses can include drawings, questions the students have, definitions of words, or other reactions the students have to the paragraph.

Did You Know?
Some scientists think that the worms *Alvinella pomejana,* which live around hydrothermal vents, may be the most heat-tolerant animals on Earth. These worms live in water that is about 149 degrees Fahrenheit. Some of the worms have survived temperatures as high as 175 degrees Fahrenheit. Scientists are investigating how the worms survive these conditions.

Activity
Encourage students to make drawings of some of the organisms that live around hydrothermal vents. For example, they might draw giant tube worms, giant white clams, crabs, snails without shells, mats of white bacteria, and so on.

Outside Resources
Literature
The Magic School Bus on the Ocean Floor by Joanna Cole. Scholastic, 1992.

Ocean: Eyewitness Books by Miranda Macquitty. Dorling Kindersley, 1995.

Internet
Extreme 2000: Voyage to the Deep
www.ocean.udel.edu/deepsea/

Ocean Adventure: From Deep Sea to Deep Space
library.thinkquest.org/18828/

If You Have Time...
Skill 21 Options

Research
- Have interested students find out more about the organisms that live near hydrothermal vents.
- Interested students might want to research the submersibles used to investigate hydrothermal vents.
- Students can research the locations of hydrothermal vents around the world. Then students can plot these locations on a map.

Skill Help
If students are having trouble understanding what the content of a learning log entry should be, engage them in a dialogue about another reading passage of science content. Model for them the various options for response, such as questions, related ideas, and reactions. Jot these down on the board. Then show how they might be connected in the conversational tone of a learning log entry.

43

Skill 22
HOW TO
Write a Paragraph

National Parks in Trouble

At a Glance
Students will learn how to write a persuasive paragraph by examining problems facing national parks.

Objectives
- Know what a persuasive paragraph is.
- Understand the steps in writing a persuasive paragraph.
- Summarize the problems faced by national parks.
- Write a persuasive paragraph in which a solution is given to a problem in a national park.

Reduced Student Pages
Teacher's Guide p. 124

Skills Workbook
For help writing a paragraph, use *Skills Workbook* pages 43–44.

Correlation to Standards
Content Standard F: Changes in environments

Content Standard F: Science and technology in local challenges

More About
Yosemite National Park
Located on the western border of the Sierra Nevada Mountains in central California, Yosemite National Park has cascading waterfalls, beautiful meadows, and forests that include groves of ancient sequoia trees. The park is a sanctuary for many kinds of wildlife, including mule deer and black bears.

Answers
Use This Skill, Student Edition p. 107
To evaluate style and mechanics, see *Teacher's Guide* pages xiv–1. Use the following scoring rubric for content.

3 The writer provides a persuasive argument supported by facts. The writing is well crafted and easy to follow. Ideas are complete.

2 The content is somewhat persuasive, but some important points or facts have been omitted. Organization could be somewhat improved.

1 Paragraph is not persuasive and/or does not stay on the subject. It does not show any evidence of organization and is difficult to understand. Ideas are incomplete and confusing.

If You Have Time...
Skill 22 Options

Skill Link
Students must be able to tell fact from opinion when writing persuasive paragraphs. For further help with this skill, see **Skill 13: How to Tell Fact from Opinion** on *Student Edition* pages 62–67.

Skill Help
To help students who are struggling to write persuasive paragraphs, explain that writing a persuasive paragraph is similar to presenting a case as a lawyer before a jury. A lawyer can't simply state an opinion. The lawyer must provide facts and evidence to convince the jury to take his or her side. Explain to students that in writing persuasive paragraphs, they should back up their opinions with facts. The facts are the evidence that can convince a reader to believe the opinions presented.

Outside Resources
Literature
Grand Canyon (National Parks Series) by Jan Mell. Crestwood House, 1988.
Letters Home From Yosemite by Lisa Halvorsen. Blackbirch Marketing, 2000.
Internet
National Park Service
www.nps.gov

Discussion
Discuss the example paragraph on *Student Edition* page 106 asking students to state the opinion and the facts that support it. Ask students if they agree with the opinion. What other solutions can they think of? What facts might they use to support their opinion? Point out that a problem might have several possible solutions.

Research
Interested students can read about the early history of Yosemite National Park. Students can research the role conservationists such as John Muir and Frederick Law Olmsted played in preserving Yosemite.

Skill 23
HOW TO
Write an Outline

Natural Resources

At a Glance
Students will learn how to write an outline by reading about natural resources.

Objectives
- Recognize the parts of an outline.
- Understand the steps in writing an outline.
- Describe renewable and nonrenewable natural resources.
- Write an outline on the advantages and disadvantages of coal.

Reduced Student Pages
Teacher's Guide pp. 125–126

Skills Workbook
For more practice writing an outline, use *Skills Workbook* pages 45–46.

Correlation to Standards
Content Standard D: Properties of earth materials

Content Standard F: Types of resources

More About
Nonrenewable Resources
One component of air pollution is carbon dioxide, a gas released from the burning of fossil fuels such as coal, oil, and natural gas. Twenty percent of carbon dioxide in the air comes from burning gas in automobiles. There are many simple ways people can reduce air pollution from cars. Keeping a car well maintained will result in using nine percent less gasoline. Walking, riding bicycles, and carpooling also help reduce air pollution and conserve nonrenewable natural resources.

Answers
Use This Skill, Student Edition p. 113

Students' outlines may vary. Possible outline:

The Advantages and Disadvantages of Using Coal

I. Advantages

    A. Creates energy when burned

    B. Can be transported easily

    C. Plentiful supplies

    D. Mining provides jobs

II. Disadvantages

    A. Causes air pollution

    B. Mining erodes land

    C. Mining coal can pollute water

    D. Difficult to mine

    E. Mining can be a dangerous job

If You Have Time...
Skill 23 Options

Skill Link
To help students with finding the main idea, see **Skill 14: How to Find the Main Idea** on *Student Edition* pages 68–71. For more information on taking notes, see **Skill 15: How to Take Notes** on *Student Edition* pages 72–77.

Outside Resources
Literature
The Atlas of Endangered Resources by Steve Pollock. Checkmark Books, 1995.
Earth Book for Kids: Activities to Help Heal the Environment by Linda Schwartz. Learning Works, 1990.
The Encyclopedia of the Environment by Stephen Kellert and Matthew Black. Franklin Watts, Inc., 1999.
Internet
Energy Information Administration Kid's Page
www.eia.doe.gov/kids/
Energy Quest
www.energy.ca.gov/education/

Did You Know?
Before miners had the monitoring equipment used today, coal miners often used canaries to test the purity of the air in the mines. A canary kept in a cage will show signs of distress due to carbon monoxide much sooner than a person. If a canary stopped singing or showed signs of sickness, the miners would know that the levels of carbon dioxide in the mines were unsafe and leave the mine.

Activity
Have students think about why conserving natural resources is important and brainstorm ways they can conserve natural resources. Then they can make informative posters or brochures showing their favorite conservation ideas.

Skill 24
HOW TO
Write a Summary

Are There Microbes in Your Future?

At a Glance
Students will learn how to write a summary as they read about microbiology and microbiologists.

Objectives
- Identify the main ideas in a reading passage.
- Recognize the purposes and uses of a summary.
- Understand what microbiologists do and how a person can pursue a career in microbiology.
- Write a summary of a reading passage.

Reduced Student Pages
Teacher's Guide pp. 126–127

Skills Workbook
For help in writing summaries, use *Skills Workbook* pages 47–48.

Correlation to Standards
Content Standard C: Organisms and environments

More About
Microbiology
The invention of the microscope was the first step that led to the discovery of germs. Even after the discovery of germs, the scientific community regarded these microbes as harmless curiosities. It would be the second half of the nineteenth century before the study of germs became known as microbiology.

Answers
Use This Skill, Student Edition p. 119
To evaluate style and mechanics, see *Teacher's Guide* pages xiv–1. Use the following scoring rubric for content.

Content Ideas and Organization

3 The summary contains all the main points of the reading. The summary does not contain unimportant details. The writer has accurately restated the main points without copying phrases.

2 The summary presents most of the major points, but one is missing. Occasionally an inaccurate or unnecessary detail is included. The writer occasionally copies phrases or incorrectly paraphrases.

1 The summary is inaccurate or difficult to follow. The main points are missing or lost among insignificant details. The writer copies large portions from the original.

Did You Know?
Scientists at California Polytechnic University revived a prehistoric bacterium from an extinct bee that was preserved in amber. The bacterium had remained dormant for 25 million years.

Outside Resources
Literature

Germs: Mysterious Microorganisms by Don Nardo. Lucent Books, Inc., 1991.

I Know How We Fight Germs by Kate Rowan. Candlewick Press, 1999.

Internet

Microbes in the News
www.commtechlab.msu.edu/sites/dlc-me/news/news.html

Research
- Have interested students research early pioneers in the field of microbiology such as Antony van Leeuwenhoek, Edward Jenner, Louis Pasteur, Robert Koch, Joseph Lister, Julius Richard Petri, Paul Ehrlich, Walter Reed, and Alexander Fleming.

- Interested students might want to research beneficial microbes that combat disease and reduce pollution.

If You Have Time...
Skill 24 Options

Skill Link
Finding the main ideas in a reading passage is an important part of writing a summary. For more information about finding the main idea, refer students to **Skill 14: How to Find the Main Idea** on *Student Edition* pages 68–71.

Skill Help
If students struggle to use their own words when writing their summaries, suggest that they try putting away the original after they read it carefully. Then they can write their summaries based on what they remember. They can then look at the original again as they revise and edit their summaries.

Skill 25
HOW TO
Write a Description

Yellowstone's Hot Springs

At a Glance
Students will learn how to write a description by writing about the hot springs at Yellowstone National Park.

Objectives
- Identify and use describing words.
- Understand how to write a description.
- Describe the characteristics of hot springs, geysers, mud pots, and fumaroles.
- Write a description of one of the geothermal wonders from Yellowstone National Park.

Reduced Student Pages
Teacher's Guide pp. 128–129

Skills Workbook
For help writing a description, use *Skills Workbook* pages 49–50.

Correlation to Standards
Content Standard D: Properties of earth materials

More About
Yellowstone's Hot Springs
Yellowstone, the first national park in the United States, was established in 1872. Yellowstone is famous for its natural wonders, including hot springs and geysers. Of the more than 3,000 hot springs in Yellowstone, Mammoth Hot Springs is arguably the most famous. Its hot waters contain limestone deposits, which over time have formed a series of terraces at the site. Each terrace is a different color, supplied by the algae that grow there, ranging from yellow to brown to terra cotta. Reflections from the pool's bottom give the clear water a blue tint.

Answers
Use This Skill, Student Edition p. 125
To evaluate style and mechanics, see *Teacher's Guide* pages xiv–1. Use the following scoring rubric for content.

3 Description provides a clear and comprehensive picture that is interesting and informative. Writer has appealed to several senses and uses descriptive language well.

2 Description is adequate but predictable. Writing contains little descriptive language and few words that appeal to the senses.

1 The description is confusing, inaccurate, or incomplete. Little attempt has been made to use descriptive language or words that appeal to the senses. Paragraph is hard to follow.

If You Have Time...
Skill 25 Options

Activity
Have students make colorful and descriptive travel brochures about Yellowstone National Park. Students can describe the many geothermal wonders that visitors can see if they visit the park. Encourage students to include artwork in the brochures as well.

Outside Resources
Literature
Earth's Fiery Fury by Sandra Downs. Twenty First Century Books, 2000.
Yellowstone National Park by David Petersen. Children's Press, 2001.
Internet
The Geyser Observation and Study Association
www.geyserstudy.org
Yellowstone National Park
www.nps.gov/yell/index.htm
Yellowstone: America's Sacred Wilderness
www.pbs.org/edens/yellowstone/

Skill Help
To help students write their descriptions, have them list the five senses (sight, sound, taste, touch, smell) and then write one description for each of the senses. They can use these notes as they write their paragraphs.

Did You Know?
Most buildings in Iceland are heated by geothermal energy because Iceland has an abundance of geothermal activity. Iceland has more hot springs than any other country in the world.

Skill Link
If students need additional help organizing their paragraphs, refer them to **Skill 23: How to Write an Outline** on *Student Edition* pages 108–113.

Skill 26
HOW TO
Write a Comparison/Contrast

Improving Technology Improves Health

At a Glance
Students will learn how to write a comparison/contrast paragraph by reading about prostheses.

Objectives
- Define *compare* and *contrast.*
- Explain how to write a comparison/contrast paragraph.
- Identify similarities and differences between modern prostheses and prostheses from the past.
- Write a comparison/contrast based on two similar pictures.

Reduced Student Pages
Teacher's Guide pp. 129–130

Skills Workbook
For help in writing a comparison/contrast, use **Skills Workbook** pages 51–52.

Correlation to Standards
Content Standard E: Understanding about science and technology

Content Standard F: Personal health

More About
The Paralympic Games
First started in 1948 as a sports competition for people with spinal cord injuries, the Paralympic Games have evolved through the years to include people with many different disabilities. The Paralympics follow the Olympic Games and often use the same venues.

Answers
Use This Skill, Student Edition p. 131
To evaluate style and mechanics, see *Teacher's Guide* pages xiv–1. Use the following scoring rubric for content.

Content: Ideas and Organization

3 The topic sentence clearly identifies the two topics being compared and contrasted. The body of the paragraph is well organized and easy to follow. Signal words and adjectives are used appropriately to signify qualities that are the same or different. The details used to compare and contrast the pictures make the writing interesting.

2 I can easily tell what is being compared and contrasted, but the paragraph includes only one or two points and lacks interest.

1 The paragraph is missing a topic sentence. The paragraph includes few details and is poorly organized.

If You Have Time...
Skill 26 Options

Skill Link
For help comparing and contrasting, refer students to **Skill 11: How to Compare and Contrast** on *Student Edition* pages 54–57.

Research
Have students research medical advances that have improved people's lives such as the development of vaccines and antibiotics, use and improvement of anesthesia, the invention of X-ray technology, MRI and CT scans, and organ transplants.

Outside Resources
Literature
Just What the Doctor Ordered: The History of American Medicine by Brandon Marie Miller. Lerner Publications Company, 1997.

Medical Advances (20th Century Inventions) by Steve Parker. Raintree/Steck Vaughn, 1998.

100 Medical Milestones That Shaped World History by Ruth DeJauregui. Bluewood Books, 1998.

Skill Help
To help students who have difficulty writing comparison/contrast paragraphs, have students try comparing and contrasting objects, people, or ideas with which they are more familiar. They can compare and contrast sports, games, foods, movies, and so on.

Did You Know?
People with prostheses have climbed Mount Everest, run marathons, competed in countless sports, modeled professionally, played on professional sports teams, worked as stunt people in movies and television, and have achieved many other accomplishments.

Skill 27
HOW TO
Write about a Process

Glass: A "Super Cool Matter"

At a Glance
Students will learn how to write about a process by reading about glassblowing.

Objectives
- Understand how to write about a process.
- Learn how to use sequence words to explain the steps in a process.
- Recognize the sequence of steps used in blowing glass.
- Write about a cooking process.

Reduced Student Pages
Teacher's Guide p. 131

Skills Workbook
For more help writing about a process, use **Skills Workbook** pages 53–54.

Correlation to Standards
Content Standard B: Properties of objects and materials

More About
How Glass is Made
For thousands of years, people have made glass using the same process. First a furnace is heated to more than 2,200 °F. Next silica (white sand), sodium oxide (soda), and calcium oxide (crushed limestone) are mixed together. This crystalline mixture is put into a pot in the furnace where it stays until it melts. The heat changes the mixture into a syrupy liquid that will no longer form crystals. Finally the melted glass is taken from the furnace and shaped into objects.

Scoring Rubric
Use this Skill, Student Edition p. 135
To evaluate style and mechanics, see *Teacher's Guide* pages xiv–1. Use the following scoring rubric for content.

3 The student has crafted a well-written paragraph. The steps are logical and easy to follow and the student has incorporated smooth transitions and sequence words that help me move from step to step.

2 The paragraph is well organized and easy to follow, although few details are provided. A few steps were not explained clearly.

1 The paragraph is difficult to follow. The steps are not explained well or are not logical.

Skill Link
Knowing how to use descriptive language can help students write about a process. For more information on this skill, refer students to **Skill 25: How to Write a Description** on *Student Edition* pages 120–125.

Research
Students who are interested in glass might research how different kinds of glass such as stained glass, recycled glass, or specialty glass (safety glass for automobiles, optical glass, telescope, or microscope lenses) are made.

Outside Resources
Literature
Chihuly by Donald Kuspit. Harry N Abrams, 1998.

Glass: An Artist's Medium by Lucartha Kohler. Krause Publications, 1999.

See-through Zoo: How Glass Animals Are Made by Suzanne Haldane. Pantheon Books, 1984.

Internet
Corning Museum of Glass
www.cmog.org

If You Have Time...
Skill 27 Options

Did You Know?
Until about 50 B.C. glass was a rare luxury. It took several days to make one bottle by pressing glass in a mold. Glass was considered as precious as gold. When the Romans discovered glassblowing, glass became more easily produced and many glass objects could be made in a day. Soon glass became common and inexpensive.

Skill Help
To help students who have difficulty writing about a process, have them think of something that they are very comfortable doing such as explaining how to make a favorite snack or play a game. Then tell them to list the steps in order. They can use this list to write a paragraph.

Skill 28
HOW TO
Use the Library

Volcanoes

At a Glance
Students will learn how to use the library as they learn about volcanoes.

Objectives
- Learn how to select sources from a card catalog and a computer catalog.
- Use the Dewey Decimal System to locate books in a library.
- Know how to find information using the different parts of a book.
- Describe volcanoes.
- Use the library to find answers to questions about volcanoes.

Reduced Student Pages
Teacher's Guide pp. 132–133

Skills Workbook
For more practice using the library, use *Skills Workbook* pages 55–56.

Correlation to Standards
Content Standard D: Properties of earth materials

Content Standard D: Changes in earth and sky

More About
Volcanoes
The Earth's crust is made up of 15 plates that float on top of the molten rock below. Volcanoes are most likely to occur where these plates come together. A belt of volcanoes in the Pacific Ocean is called the "Ring of Fire." The Ring of Fire covers the western coast of North America and South America, the east coast of Asia, and areas north and east of Australia. Seventy-five percent of Earth's 850 active volcanoes are found in the Ring of Fire.

Answers
Use This Skill, Student Edition p. 141
Answers will vary. Students should choose one of the questions listed on *Student Edition* page 141 or write one of their own. Students should find at least one source in a library that has the answer to their question. They should include the call number and title of the source.

Activity
Have students make maps of their school library. Have students include the location of computers, card catalogs, reference books, fiction books, nonfiction books, newspapers, magazines, and videotapes.

Did You Know?
About 50 to 60 volcanoes erupt every year. Most volcanic eruptions last between 10 and 100 days.

If You Have Time...
Skill 28 Options

Research
Have students choose a volcano, such as Mount Saint Helens in Washington, Mount Fuji in Japan, Mauna Loa in Hawaii, or Mount Tambora in Indonesia, to research. Students can prepare either oral or written reports on the information they find.

Outside Resources
Literature
Earthquakes and Volcanoes by Lin Sutherland. Reader's Digest Children's Publishing, 2000.
DK Guide to Savage Earth by Trevor Day. DK Publishing, 2001.
The Volcano Disaster by Peg Kehret. Aladdin Paperbacks, 1998.

Internet
Volcano World
volcano.und.edu/
Volcano Live
www.volcanolive.com/contents.html

Skill Help
To help students understand where materials are located in a library, take them on a tour of your school library or ask your school librarian to show students where different materials are located.

Skill 29
HOW TO
Write a Report

Pedal Power

At a Glance
Students will learn how to write a report as they read about the development of bicycles.

Objectives
- Learn how to gather information and take notes for a report.
- Learn how to organize information for a report.
- Learn how to write a report and compose a bibliography.
- Describe the development of the bicycle chronologically.
- Write a report about one aspect of bicycling.

Reduced Student Pages
Teacher's Guide pp. 133–134

Skills Workbook
For more help writing a report, use **Skills Workbook** pages 57–58.

Correlation to Standards
Content Standard E: Understanding about science and technology

Content Standard F: Personal health

More About
Bicycles
The earliest bicycles were propelled by foot, were made of wood, were loud, and were most likely uncomfortable. Over time, improvements were made, including pedals, handlebars that could be used to steer, brakes, and pneumatic tires. Today's bikes have developed into machines that are comfortable, practical, safe, and lightweight.

Answers
Use This Skill, Student Edition p. 147
To evaluate style and mechanics, see *Teacher's Guide* pages xiv–1. Use the following scoring rubric for content.

Content: Ideas and Organization
3 The report is well researched and organized. The report is interesting and has a clear beginning, middle, and ending, making it easy to follow. The report includes a bibliography that lists the sources used and is formatted correctly.

2 The report is well researched but lacks organization. The report lacks interest. A bibliography is included but it has some mistakes in formatting.

1 The report is poorly researched and not organized. The student's thoughts are not clearly worded or it appears that the student copied from sources. The student did not include a bibliography.

Activity
- Have students make posters depicting various aspects of bicycle safety.
- Have students make time lines showing how bicycles changed over time.

Research
Have interested students research other modes of transportation that have changed over time. For example, students can research improvements in automobile and airline safety that have taken place over the years.

Did You Know?
In 1979 a Belgian bicycle was built that seated 35 people, was 67 feet long, and weighed 2,425 pounds.

Outside Resources
Literature
Amazing Bikes by Trevor Lord. Alfred A. Knopf, Inc., 1992.

Bicycles by Arlene Erlbach. Lerner Publications Company, 1994.

Safety on Your Bicycle by Joanne Mattern. ABDO Publishing Company, 1999.

World on Wheels: An Illustrated History of the Bicycle and Its Relatives by Ruth Calif. Random House Value Publishers, 1986.

If You Have Time...
Skill 29 Options

Discussion
The American Academy of Pediatrics strongly recommends that people wear helmets while riding a bicycle. Ask students to think of their own reasons why people should wear bike helmets.

Skill Link
For further help in gathering information and taking notes for a report, refer to **Skill 15: How to Take Notes** on *Student Edition* pages 72–77 and **Skill 28: How to Use the Library** on *Student Edition* pages 136–141.

Skill 30
HOW TO
Prepare a Display

Telescopes

At a Glance
Students will learn how to prepare a display by reading about telescopes.

Objectives
- Define *display*.
- Identify the steps in making a display.
- Demonstrate how a display shows what someone has learned.
- Analyze the organizational structure of a display about hand lenses used as a telescope.
- Create a three-panel display about a science topic.

Reduced Student Pages
Teacher's Guide pp. 135–136

Skills Workbook
For more practice preparing a display, use *Skills Workbook* pages 59–60.

Correlation to Standards
Content Standard A: Understanding about scientific inquiry

Content Standard B: Light, heat, electricity, and magnetism

More About
Telescopes and Mirrors
Sir Isaac Newton discovered problems with the refracting telescopes of the seventeenth century. The light coming from the stars was bent by the glass lenses, much like light coming through a prism. False colors appeared around the stars. Newton developed a reflecting telescope that used two mirrors to collect and focus the light. The front of the mirror that collected the light was curved (concave), like the inside of a spoon. It focused the light just like a lens focuses light. This solved the problem of seeing false colors.

Scoring Rubric
Use this Skill, Student Edition p. 153
To evaluate style and mechanics, see *Teacher's Guide* pages xiv–1. Use the following rubric for content.

3 The display is attractive and organized. The display clearly shows what the student learned. Headings and titles are large and neatly written or typed. The display includes attractive visuals.

2 The display includes all the necessary elements but shows a lack of organization or neatness. It is not clear what the student learned in doing the project.

1 The display is missing one or more elements. The display is poorly organized. It is not clear what the student learned.

Research
Interested students might want to research the history of the Hubble Space Telescope and accomplishments that have occurred since the telescope was launched in 1990.

Did You Know?
Huge telescopes used by astronomers at observatories around the world must move to counteract the motion caused by the rotation of Earth. They move in order to keep distant objects continuously in view. The telescopes pivot on a vertical axis and horizontal axis. The telescopes are moved by computer-controlled motors.

Outside Resources
Literature
Janice VanCleave's Guide to More of the Best Science Fair Projects by Janice VanCleave. John Wiley & Sons Inc., 2000.

Internet
The Ultimate Science Fair Resource: Display Boards
www.scifair.org/articles/display.shtml

National Geographic—Star Journey
www.nationalgeographic.com/features/97/stars/index.html

NASA Goddard Space Flight Center: The Hubble Project
hubble.gsfc.nasa.gov/

If You Have Time...
Skill 30 Options

Skill Link
Students may want to make graphs and tables to include in their displays. To help students with these skills, refer them to **Skill 33: How to Make a Table** on *Student Edition* pages 166–169 and **Skill 35: How to Make a Line Graph** on *Student Edition* pages 174–179.

Skill Help
If students struggle to make an attractive display, suggest that they sketch their ideas on a piece of paper before making the display. Remind them to write or type their headings and titles so that they are large and easy to read. Suggest that students try putting black paper or a single color behind their text and pictures to make an attractive border.

Skill 31

HOW TO
Do a Survey

Cleaning Up the Environment

At a Glance
Students will learn how to do a survey by reading about an environmental project.

Objectives
- Learn how to write questions for a survey.
- Understand how to collect and display survey data.
- Discover ways to turn a neighborhood eyesore into a work of art.
- Do a survey to find out which environmental project classmates prefer, and show the results in a bar graph.

Reduced Student Pages
Teacher's Guide pp. 136–137

Skills Workbook
For help doing a survey, use *Skills Workbook* pages 61–62.

Correlation to Standards
Content Standard D: Properties of earth materials

Content Standard D: Changes in earth and sky

More About
Community Gardens
Drive through the streets of Minneapolis, Minnesota, and you'll find some surprising sights. The inner city is full of community gardens. Several years ago, members of one Minneapolis community got the idea to turn a vacant lot, which was being used by gang members who were selling drugs, into a vegetable garden. The local block club got permission to improve the vacant lot from the city council. Neighbors worked together to clear the weeds and till the soil. Then they divided the lot into small gardens. Any neighbor who wanted one could have a garden. Soon everything from bok choy to sunflowers was sprouting from what used to be a neighborhood eyesore. Neighbors got to know each other and learned to work together as they planted and weeded their gardens. Now gardens are popular throughout the city.

Answers
Use This Skill, Student Edition p. 159
Students' surveys will vary. Students should write out their survey questions. They should survey a large group of their classmates and tally the responses correctly. They should show the data in a neat and easy-to-read bar graph.

Did You Know?
With careful planning, you can help save and care for animals in your community garden by choosing plants that provide them with natural food and shelter. Hummingbirds, for example, are attracted to red morning glories. A bird feeder or a birdbath will draw many other kinds of birds. Chipmunks and rabbits will often visit gardens if walls and shrubs are present.

Outside Resources
Literature
Garden by Robert Maass. Henry Holt and Company, 1998.
The Garden of Happiness by Erika Tamar. Harcourt, 1996.
Kid's Garden: The Anytime, Anyplace Guide to Sowing and Growing Fun by Avery Hart and Paul Mantell. Williamson Publishing, 1996.

Internet
My First Garden
www.urbanext.uiuc.edu/firstgarden/
Aggie Horticulture: Just for Kids
aggie-horticulture.tamu.edu/kindergarden/index.html

If You Have Time...
Skill 31 Options

Discussion
Discuss with students other ways that people can improve their schools, neighborhoods, and communities. Have students brainstorm a list of actions they can take to make a difference.

Skill Link
Knowing how to collect data and how to read a bar graph are important skills when taking a survey. For further help with this skill, see **Skill 5: How to Collect Data** on *Student Edition* pages 22–27.

Skill 32
HOW TO
Read a Time Line

Rockets!

At a Glance
Students will learn to read a time line by learning about rockets.

Objectives
- Define *time line.*
- Analyze the organizational structure of a time line.
- Recognize the chronological order of key events in rocket history.
- Use information from a time line to answer written questions.

Reduced Student Pages
Teacher's Guide p. 138

Skills Workbook
For more practice reading time lines, use *Skills Workbook* pages 63–64.

Correlation to Standards
Content Standard E: Understanding about science and technology

Content Standard G: Science as a human endeavor

More About
Rocket Science
The scientific foundations for the science of rocketry were laid by Sir Isaac Newton in his three laws of physical motion: (1) an object will move only if a force is applied to it, then will continue at the same speed and direction unless a force is applied to change it; (2) the amount an object slows down or speeds up varies with the mass of the object and the size of the force; and (3) for every action, there is an equal and opposite reaction. When a rocket is launched, the blast of hot gases pushing against the air from its tail section propels it into the air. When it reaches space, where there is no air to push on, the rocket continues to be propelled by action and reaction between the rocket and the gases from the engine. The escaping exhaust gases are the action. The forward thrust is the reaction and the rocket moves forward.

Answers
Use this Skill, Student Edition p. 165

1. 1957

2. four months

Research
Students interested in rockets might want to study some of the pioneers in the development of rockets, such as Konstantin Tsiolkovsky, Robert Goddard, and Hermann Oberth. Students also might want to research the space race between the Soviet Union and the United States, which began after the Soviet Union launched the first satellite, *Sputnik I,* into space.

Activity
Have students create their own balloon rockets. First students should cut a long piece of string. Then they should thread the string through a drinking straw. Next they should inflate a long balloon and put a clothespin on the neck of the balloon to keep the air from escaping. Next they should tape the balloon to the straw. Lastly the students should hang the string across the room. To launch the balloon, the students simply need to take the clothespin off the balloon.

Outside Resources
Literature
Cosmic Science: Over 40 Gravity-Defying, Earth-Orbiting, Space-Cruising Activities for Kids by Jim Wiese. John Wiley & Sons, 1997.

The Everything Kids Space Book: All about rockets, moon landings, Mars, and more plus space activities you can do at home! by Kathiann M. Kowalski. Adams Media Corp., 2000.

The History of Rockets by Ron Miller. Franklin Watts, Inc., 1999.

Internet
A Brief History of Rocketry
http://science.ksc.nasa.gov/history/rocket-history.txt

Brief History of Rockets
http://teacherlink.ed.usu.edu/TLresources/longterm/NASA/html/rockets/history/history.html

If You Have Time…
Skill 32 Options

Did You Know?
Rockets fired by British ships against the United States in 1812 inspired Francis Scott Key to write about the "the rockets' red glare." These words would later become part of "The Star-Spangled Banner."

Discussion
Ask students if individuals should be able to pay money to travel in the space shuttle or stay in a space station. Students can discuss the advantages and disadvantages of space tourism.

Skill 33
HOW TO Make a Table

Going, Going, Gone?

At a Glance
Students will learn how to make a table by comparing information about endangered animals.

Objectives
- Understand that a table is a way to present and compare information so that it is organized and easy to read.
- Define *endangered.*
- Identify numbers and locations of specific endangered animals in the wild.
- Make a table that compares the number of endangered animals in the United States with the number in the rest of the world.

Reduced Student Pages
Teacher's Guide p. 139

Skills Workbook
For more practice in making a table, use *Skills Workbook* pages 65–66.

Correlation to Standards
Content Standard C: Organisms and environments

More About
Endangered Species
In 1966, Congress passed the Endangered Species Preservation Act. This act authorized the compiling of a list of endangered species and the development of a program to conserve them. In 1969, a law was passed to prohibit importing of endangered species. In 1973, legislation was enacted that contained important changes from the previous two laws. First, it stated that every plant and animal could be protected instead of just certain groups. Second, the species eligible now included not only species but also subspecies. Finally, the legislation protected not only endangered species but also threatened species: those that were likely to become endangered.

Answers
Use This Skill, Student Edition p. 169
Students should set up their tables like the example on *Student Edition* page 169. The information in the table should appear as follows:

Row 1: Mammals; 63; 251; 314
Row 2: Birds; 78; 175; 253
Row 3: Reptiles; 14; 64; 78
Row 4: Fish; 70; 11; 81
Row 5: Amphibians; 10; 8; 18

Discussion
Have students discuss the causes of animal and plant endangerment. Then ask students to develop solutions to some of the problems.

Research
- Have interested students research how loss of animal habitats affects both animals and humans. Ask students to provide examples of animals that are now competing with humans for living spaces and resources. Examples include deer and rabbits eating vegetation in people's yards; raccoons and bears getting into garbage; and squirrels and raccoons building nests in the attics of houses and other buildings.
- Some students may be interested in investigating endangered plants and animals in your area. Have the students share their findings with the class.

Outside Resources
Literature
And Then There Was One: The Mysteries of Extinction by Margery Facklam. Little Brown & Company, 1993.

There's an Owl in the Shower by Jean Craighead George. HarperCollins Juvenile Books, 1995.

Will We Miss Them? Endangered Species by Alexandra Wright. Charlesbridge Publishing, 1993.

Internet
American Museum of Natural History—Endangered! Exploring a World at Risk
www.amnh.org/nationalcenter/Endangered/

If You Have Time...
Skill 33 Options

Skill Link
Students often use tables to help them collect data. For more information about collecting data, refer students to **Skill 5: How to Collect Data** on *Student Edition* pages 22–27.

Did You Know?
Since 1973, six species have been removed from the federal endangered and threatened species list because their populations have recovered. Seven species have been removed from the list because they became extinct.

67

Skill 34
HOW TO
Read a Bar Graph

Up in Smoke

At a Glance
Students will learn how to read a bar graph as they read about the effects of smoking.

Objectives
- Learn how to read a bar graph.
- Understand how smoking cigarettes affects the body.
- Read a bar graph that shows information about smoking-related diseases.
- Use a bar graph to answer questions about why people choose not to smoke.

Reduced Student Pages
Teacher's Guide p. 140

Skills Workbook
For more practice reading a bar graph, use *Skills Workbook* pages 67–68.

Correlation to Standards
Content Standard F: Personal health

More About
Smoking
There is no safe tobacco. All tobacco contains nicotine, so all tobacco is addictive. Many young smokers think they will be able to quit before smoking affects their health, but smoking begins to affect one's health with the first cigarette. Early effects include shortness of breath, wheezing, coughing, nausea, and dizziness. Children who smoke are eight times more likely to smoke marijuana and three times more likely to use alcohol than their nonsmoking peers. Trying to quit smoking causes withdrawal symptoms, such as anxiety, difficulty concentrating, restlessness, and decreased heart rate, making it very difficult for most people to quit smoking.

Answers
Use This Skill, Student Edition p. 173
1. Don't want to become addicted
2. Don't want teeth to turn yellow

Did You Know?
Smoke contains 4,000 chemicals, including carbon monoxide, formaldehyde, ammonia, arsenic, and nickel. Forty of the chemicals are carcinogenic.

Outside Resources
Literature
Everything You Need to Know About Smoking by Elizabeth Keyishian. The Rosen Publishing Group, Inc., 2000.

Tobacco and Your Mouth: The Incredibly Disgusting Story by Michael A. Sommers. The Rosen Publishing Group, Inc., 2000.

Internet
The Surgeon General's Report for Kids about Smoking
www.cdc.gov/tobacco/sgr/sgr4kids/6facts.htm

Activity
- Have students do additional research about the dangers of smoking and make antismoking posters.

- Have students role-play situations in which they may be tempted to start smoking. Encourage them to come up with different ways to say "no" to smoking.

- Explain to students that each cigarette shortens a person's life by 5 to 20 minutes. Have students calculate how much time would be lost over a lifetime if a person, beginning at age 18, smokes a pack (20 cigarettes) a day for 10, 20, or 30 years. Change the beginning age, number of cigarettes, and number of years smoking to have students calculate again. Also have students calculate the cost of cigarettes, using the same information and today's cost of cigarettes.

If You Have Time...
Skill 34 Options

Skill Help
To help students understand how to read bar graphs, give students much additional practice in reading them. Look for bar graphs in newspapers and magazines. As a class, construct bar graphs about class data (such as birthdays, pets, and favorite foods) and read the bar graphs together.

Discussion
Have students discuss nonsmoking facilities such as stores, restaurants, public transportation, and so on. Ask students if they think these facilities are necessary and fair. Have students discuss the benefits and drawbacks of these kinds of places.

Skill 35
HOW TO
Make a Line Graph

Tracking the Temperature

At a Glance
Students will learn how to make a line graph showing how temperatures change over time.

Objectives
- Identify parts of a line graph.
- Understand how to make a line graph to show how something changes over time.
- Make a line graph based on information provided in a table.

Reduced Student Pages
Teacher's Guide pp. 141–142

Skills Workbook
For more practice making a line graph, use *Skills Workbook* pages 69–70.

Correlation to Standards
Content Standard D: Changes in earth and sky

More About
Temperature and Weather
Weather is the condition of the atmosphere at a particular time and place. When changes in the condition of the atmosphere occur, we experience different types of weather systems. Weather can be described by the temperature, humidity, precipitation, wind, and pressure.

Answers
Use this Skill, Student Edition p. 179
Student line graphs may vary slightly. Graphs should have a title and labels. Graphs should include points (based on data provided in the table on **Student Edition** page 179) plotted on the graph as well as a line connecting the points.

Did You Know?
The record for the highest temperature in the United States is in California's Death Valley with a temperature of 134 °F in 1913.

Activity
Have students choose a city in the United States or a city in another country and collect data about the temperature or amount of rainfall in that city. Students can organize their data in a table and then make line graphs to show the information.

Outside Resources
Literature
National Audubon Society First Field Guide Weather by Jonathan D. Kahl. Scholastic Trade, 1998.

Internet
Make Your Own Weather Station
www.fi.edu/weather/todo/todo.html

The Weather Underground
www.weatherunderground.com

If You Have Time...
Skill 35 Options

Skill Link
Students may need to review how to make tables before making a line graph. Refer students to **Skill 33: How to Make a Table** on *Student Edition* pages 166–169.

Skill Help
To help students who are having difficulty making line graphs, have them look for examples of line graphs in newspapers and magazines. Then have them label the parts of the line graph including the title, labels, number scale, and so on.

Skill 36
HOW TO
Read a Circle Graph

Conserving Water

At a Glance
Students will learn how to read a circle graph by reading about water conservation.

Objectives
- Understand the purposes of circle graphs.
- Learn how to interpret circle graphs.
- Examine reasons to conserve water.
- Read a circle graph that shows how much water a girl uses in one day.

Reduced Student Pages
Teacher's Guide pp. 142–143

Skills Workbook
For more practice reading a circle graph, use *Skills Workbook* pages 71–72.

Correlation to Standards
Content Standard F: Types of resources

Content Standard F: Changes in environments

More About
Conserving Water
There are many ways that people can conserve water. Families who use low-flow faucet aerators can save thousands of gallons of water a year. When this device is attached to a water faucet, it adds air to the water. The water flow seems the same, but half of it is air. Families can also install displacement devices in their toilet tanks. This reduces the amount of water the tank will hold. Families who do this can save 1 to 2 gallons of water per flush. That adds up to between 3,000 to 5,000 gallons a year. Turning off the water when doing everyday activities also makes a big difference.

Answers
Use This Skill, Student Edition p. 183
1. How much water Tracey used in one day
2. 12 gallons
3. 1 gallon
4. 0.6 gallons
5. 140 gallons
6. taking a shower
7. 43 gallons
8. Answers will vary. Possible answers include: Turning off the water while brushing teeth; turning off water when soaping up in the shower; installing low-flow aerators; and so on.

Skill Help
To give students additional practice reading circle graphs, have them search for and collect examples of circle graphs from magazines, newspapers, and books. Display the circle graphs on a bulletin board and have students practice reading them. You might want to list several questions for each graph and challenge students to find the answers by reading the graph.

Outside Resources
Literature
A Cool Drink of Water by Barbara Kerley. National Geographic Society, 2001.
Drought by Catherine Chambers. Heinemann Library, 2000.

Internet
Water in the City
www.fi.edu/city/water/
Water Science for Schools
ga.water.usgs.gov/edu/index.html
What on Earth Do You Know About Water?
www.epa.gov/gmpo/edresources/water_5.html

If You Have Time...
Skill 36 Options

Activity
Challenge students to keep track of their own water usage for a day on a chart similar to the one on **Student Edition** page 182. Then you might want to have students make circle graphs to show their water usage. Students can compare their graphs and talk about ways to conserve water.

Discussion
Have students compare circle graphs with tables, line graphs, and bar graphs. You might want to display data from one of the circle graphs in the lesson in another format. Ask students which graph they prefer for that information and why. Discuss how different kinds of graphs are useful for displaying different kinds of data.

Did You Know?
Although it's a good idea to save water, it's not a good idea to cut down on time spent washing your hands. Doctors suggest that we wash our hands with soap and water for at least 30 seconds to get rid of germs.

Skill 37
HOW TO
Make a Diagram

Amazing Insects

At a Glance
Students will learn how to make a diagram as they read about insects.

Objectives
- Understand the purpose of diagrams.
- Identify different types of diagrams.
- Describe characteristics of insects.
- Define *metamorphosis.*
- Make a diagram showing the life cycle of a dragonfly.

Reduced Student Pages
Teacher's Guide pp. 143–144

Skills Workbook
For more practice making diagrams, use *Skills Workbook* pages 73–74.

Correlation to Standards
Content Standard C: The characteristics of organisms

Content Standard C: Life cycles of organisms

More About
Observing Insects
When an insect is kept for a limited time for observation and closer study, a few simple guidelines will insure that it stays safe and healthy. To house the insect, punch holes in the lid of a jar or plastic container. Make a comfortable environment for the insect by placing a small dish in the container with a damp sponge or a paper towel to provide some moisture. Provide grass and leaves as well as some twigs for a climbing insect. If the insect is to be observed over a longer period of time, do some research and provide appropriate food. Release the insect back into the environment where you found it at the end of the observation.

Answers
Use This Skill, Student Edition p. 189
Diagrams will vary slightly, but students should draw a cycle diagram showing the incomplete metamorphosis of a dragonfly in the following order: dragonfly egg, dragonfly nymph, and adult dragonfly.

Discussion
Have students discuss insects they have seen. Ask students to discuss ways that some insects positively affect people. Ask students to discuss negative effects of some insects.

Activity
- Take students on a walk through a neighborhood near your school or a park. Tell students to look for insects as they walk. They can draw pictures of the insects they see and then use books about insects to label them. Students can do additional research to find out more about the insects they see.

- To help students understand life cycles in more depth, order milkweed bugs, mealworms, or caterpillars from a biological supply company. Place the insects you choose inside a plastic bug cage or a jar with holes punched in the top. Be sure to include the appropriate food for the insects. Students can observe how the insects change.

Outside Resources
Literature
Insect by Laurence Mound. Alfred A. Knopf, 1990.

The Insect Book: A Basic Guide to the Collection and Care of Common Insects for Young Children by Connie Zakowski. Rainbow Books, 1997.

Insectlopedia: Poems and Paintings by Douglas Florian. Harcourt, 1998.

Roberto, the Insect Architect by Nina Laden. Chronicle Books, 2000.

Internet
Insecta Inspecta World
www.insecta-inspecta.com

USGS: Children's Butterfly Site
www.mesc.usgs.gov/resources/education/butterfly/Butterfly.shtml

If You Have Time...
Skill 37 Options

Research
Interested students might want to research different topics related to insects, such as insect groups, insect defenses, beneficial insects, insects and pesticides, and insects as a food source.

Did You Know?
The number of eggs produced by different types of insects varies widely. For example, a female spider-hunting wasp produces 20–40 eggs over her lifetime. A queen termite can produce more than ten million.

Skill 38
HOW TO
Read a Flowchart

How Storms Form

At a Glance
Students will learn how to read a flowchart that shows how storms form.

Objectives
- Identify flowcharts.
- Read flowcharts.
- Explain how storms form.
- Answer questions by analyzing a flowchart that shows how storms form.

Reduced Student Pages
Teacher's Guide p. 145

Skills Workbook
For more practice reading a flowchart, use **Skills Workbook** pages 75–76.

Correlation to Standards
Content Standard D: Changes in earth and sky

More About
Freezing Rain and Sleet
Freezing rain is rain that falls as a liquid. When the rain comes into contact with a freezing object, such as the ground, it turns to ice. The freezing rain forms a smooth coating. Freezing rain usually turns into rain or snow. Sleet is frozen or partially frozen rain that falls as ice pellets. Sleet forms when rain from a warmer layer of air passes through a freezing layer of air near Earth's surface. These hard ice pellets can hit the ground so fast that they bounce.

Answers
Use This Skill, Student Edition p. 193
1. How rainstorms, hailstorms, and snowstorms develop
2. the box on the top
3. 8
4. rainstorm, hailstorm, snowstorm
5. Droplets of water join together to form raindrops, which fall to the ground.
6. Water vapor in clouds freezes into ice crystals called snowflakes and falls to the ground.
7. Droplets of water in clouds freeze into balls of ice. Many layers of ice form on the balls. The balls of ice fall to the ground as hail.

Skill Link
A flowchart is one kind of diagram. To give students practice in making diagrams, refer students to **Skill 37: How to Make a Diagram** on *Student Edition* pages 184–189.

Skill Help
To help students who are having difficulty reading flowcharts, have them make a simple flowchart of a process they do often, such as making a sandwich, getting from home to school each day, or playing a game. Then have students trade flowcharts and read them.

If You Have Time...
Skill 38 Options

Did You Know?
The average hailstone is about $\frac{1}{4}$ inch in diameter, but many larger hailstones have been reported. Hailstones as large as 7.5 pounds reportedly fell in India in 1939; in 1986 hailstones weighing 2.5 pounds were reported in Bangladesh. A hailstone weighing 1.67 pounds and measuring 5.57 inches in diameter was reported in Kansas in 1970.

Outside Resources
Literature
Snow, Snow: Winter Poems for Children by Jane Yolen. Boyds Mills Press, 1998.
Snowflake Bentley by Jacqueline Briggs Martin. Houghton Mifflin Company, 1999.
Weather Explained: A Beginner's Guide to the Elements by Derek Elsom. Henry Holt and Company, 1997.
What Makes it Rain? The Story of a Raindrop by Keith Brandt. Troll Communications, 1989.

Skill 39
HOW TO
Make a Graphic Organizer

A Bright Idea

At a Glance
Students will learn how to make a graphic organizer by creating a concept web with information about energy efficient lightbulbs.

Objectives
- Define *graphic organizer*.
- Select graphic organizers based on information to be shown.
- Analyze organizational structure of graphic organizers.
- Identify main idea and details about energy efficient lightbulbs.
- Organize information about fluorescent lightbulbs into a concept web.

Reduced Student Pages
Teacher's Guide p. 146

Skills Workbook
For more practice making a graphic organizer, use **Skills Workbook** pages 77–78.

Correlation to Standards
Content Standard A: Understanding about scientific inquiry

Content Standard B: Light, heat, electricity, and magnetism

More About
Fluorescent Lights
Fluorescent lamps have several advantages over incandescent lightbulbs. Fluorescent lamps using 40 watts can generate as much light as a 150-watt incandescent bulb. The phosphors in fluorescent lamps can be adjusted to give off light of different qualities and they can last up to 20,000 hours longer than incandescent bulbs. Compact fluorescent lights adapted to fit traditional lightbulb sockets can last 10,000 hours or more. Switching to more efficient fluorescent lighting has helped businesses and government agencies save millions of dollars.

Answers
Use this Skill, Student Edition p. 197
Students' concept webs should include the main idea in the center of the web and details about energy efficient lightbulbs surrounding the main idea.

Discussion
Have students discuss ways to save energy such as using energy efficient lightbulbs, turning off lights when leaving the room, and so on. Ask students why saving energy is important.

Did You Know?
The filament in an incandescent lightbulb can reach a temperature of nearly 5,000 °F. The filaments in incandescent lightbulbs today are made of tungsten because of its high melting point.

Outside Resources
Literature
The Thomas Edison Book of Easy and Incredible Experiments by James G. Cook. John Wiley & Sons, Inc., 1988.

The Light Bulb and How It Changed the World (History and Science) by Michael Pollard. Facts on File, Inc., 1995.

Internet
The American Experience: Edison's Miracle of Light
www.pbs.org/wgbh/amex/edison/

The Lemelson-MIT Awards Program's Invention Dimension: Lewis H. Latimer
w3.mit.edu/invent/www/inventorsI-Q/latimer.html

If You Have Time...
Skill 39 Options

Research
Have interested students research different kinds of lighting such as incandescent lightbulbs, fluorescent lightbulbs, compact fluorescent lightbulbs, halogen lightbulbs, black lights, strobe lights, and so on.

Skill Link
Knowing how to find the main idea and take notes are important skills when learning how to make a graphic organizer. For further help, refer students to **Skill 14: How to Find the Main Idea** on *Student Edition* pages 68–71 and **Skill 15: How to Take Notes** on *Student Edition* pages 72–77.

Skill 40
HOW TO
Read a Map

The Everglades

At a Glance
Students will learn how to read a map by reading about Everglades National Park.

Objectives
- Identify the parts of a map.
- Understand the purposes of a map title, legend, compass rose, and scale.
- Read a map of Everglades National Park.
- Use a map of Everglades National Park to answer questions.

Reduced Student Pages
Teacher's Guide p. 147

Skills Workbook
For more practice reading maps, use **Skills Workbook** pages 79–80.

Correlation to Standards
Content Standard C: Organisms and environments

Content Standard F: Changes in environments

More About
The Everglades
The Everglades is actually a very slow-moving river in which saw grass proliferates. At one time, the Everglades covered nearly a third of Florida. Today the Everglades consists of 1.5 million acres or about 4,000 square miles. About one half of the original area has been drained to make useable land. The area is somewhat protected now, but the impact humans have had on the area due to building canal systems, altering riverbanks, damming nearby Lake Okeechobee, and farming continues to have a negative impact on the habitats in this area, threatening wildlife.

Answers
Use This Skill, Student Edition p. 201
1. Gulf of Mexico
2. Florida Bay
3. North
4. About 43 miles
5. Answers will vary. Possible answers include: Chekika, Long Pine Key, and Flamingo.
6. Answers will vary. Possible answers include: Chekika, Long Pine Key, Nine Mile Pond, and Flamingo.
7. East
8. About 15 miles

If You Have Time...
Skill 40 Options

Activity
Have students find out more about the Everglades and create informative travel brochures about the national park.

Outside Resources
Internet
Discover the Everglades
http://southflorida.sun-sentinel.com/everglades

Everglades National Park
www.nps.gov/ever/

Literature
Deadly Waters by Gloria Skurzynski. National Geographic Society, 1999.

Everglades by Jean Craighead George. HarperCollins Publishers, 1995.

Sawgrass Poems: A View of the Everglades by Frank Asch. Gulliver Books, 1996.

Research
- Have students find out more about the different endangered animals in the Everglades and present their findings to the class. Possible animals to research include: American crocodile, Florida manatee, Florida panther, Schaus swallowtail, snail kite, bald eagle, tree snails, and sea turtle.

- Interested students can research Ernest F. Coe, considered the "Father of the Everglades," who began arguing for the need to create a national park in the Everglades in 1928. Students can also read about Marjory Stoneman Douglas, a conservationist, who wrote the influential book *The Everglades: River of Grass* in 1947, the year the national park was established.

Skill Help
To help students become comfortable with the cardinal directions, label these directions on your classroom walls. Use these directions as reference points whenever you give students instructions. For example, put the paper on the table on the north wall, line your chairs up against the east wall, and so on.

Discussion
Discuss with students the problems that led to the creation of Everglades National Park. Ask students how they think economic needs and development can be balanced with the need for a healthy environment.

Test-Taking Strategy
Skimming a Passage

At a Glance
Students will learn how to quickly read written passages on tests.

Objectives
- Skim a passage rather than read it for content.
- Refer back to a passage to answer a question.
- Read for general meaning, not detail.

Reduced Student Pages
Teacher's Guide p. 148

Skills Workbook
For more practice skimming a passage, use *Skills Workbook* pages 81–82.

More About
Skimming a Passage
Most students make the mistake of spending too much time reading text passages that are on achievement tests. Direct instruction is required to teach students about skimming. Even though skimming seems self-evident, some students do not understand the concept. Students typically don't know when skimming should be used, and more importantly, they don't know how to do it. Take the time to help students understand the importance of skimming reading passages when time is an issue, such as during tests.

Answer
Student Edition p. 205
1. D, There are many endangered species that are helped by the 1973 act, but some species are still dying out.

If You Have Time...
Strategy Options

Activity
Have students turn to a page in a textbook or other printed material. You may wish to have all students read the same passage. Tell them that you are going to challenge them to skim a page in just ten seconds and then tell you as much about the page as they can. Start the activity by telling the students to begin and then count backward from ten slowly. At the end of the time, tell the students to stop. Have volunteers tell you as much as they can about what they have read. A variation of the activity is to preview what the students are reading and ask them a specific question about it. See how quickly they can skim the material to find what you have asked.

Skill Help
All students, no matter what their reading ability, will need some help with skimming. Some elements of skimming you should review with the students are identifying the main idea; noting but not memorizing important characters, places, dates, and such; recalling the general sequence of events; and recalling where in a passage information is located. You may also find it helpful to teach students how to skim items to identify simple versus difficult concepts, ideas, or questions.

Discussion
Skimming is not a skill that comes naturally to students. Many students, particularly those challenged by a reading, will attempt to read and memorize a test. To reinforce this test-taking strategy, you should repeat the skimming activity throughout the school year. In addition, it is worth discussing with the students the various types of reading: reading a novel for pleasure, reading directions to assemble something, reading a newspaper or magazine, and reading a reference source for information.

Test-Taking Strategy
Understanding Sequence

At a Glance
Students will learn how to understand the sequence of events in a passage.

Objectives
- Understand the meaning of *sequence*.
- Refer back to a passage or time line to answer questions.
- Work methodically.
- Analyze questions and answer choices.
- Identify keywords.

Reduced Student Pages
Teacher's Guide p. 148

Skills Workbook
For more practice understanding sequence, use **Skills Workbook** pages 83–84.

More About
Understanding Sequence
Students have more difficulty with passages that are not in chronological order than those that are in chronological order. Examples of this practice are biographies that start in the mid or late life of the subject or the description of a historical event that begins with a climax rather than at the beginning of the event's sequence. This juxtaposition of time will be challenging for readers who confuse textual sequence with temporal sequence.

Answer
Student Edition p. 207
1. A, gas bubbles form, pressure builds, volcano erupts

Skill Help

Because sequence is something students experience every day, they have few problems understanding the concept itself. On an achievement test, however, students may make mistakes by misreading questions or answer choices. Sequence-related keywords in questions and answer choices are often easy to miss. To clarify this concept, select a sample reading passage and write several practice test questions on the board. Work with the class to identify keywords, refer back to the passage, and answer the questions.

If You Have Time…
Strategy Options

Discussion

An important aspect of sequence is recognizing time and order words in a passage, in questions, and in answer choices. Discuss varied examples of these types of words with the students. Students should be able to easily recognize these words and understand what they mean in the context of the passage. In addition, it will be useful to teach students about interpolating and extrapolating within the time described in a passage. This will help students answer questions of the following type: Which of these events would have occurred after event A but before event B?

Activity

As a class or small group, have students outline on the board the typical day of a student. It will help if you give the hypothetical student a name and create a background for the student. After the day has been outlined, ask the students sequence questions about the outline. Extend the activity by asking the questions about their own day, such as, "What did you do right before you came to school?" The more specific the question, the more likely it is that students will be able to answer accurately and understand the importance of time and order words.

Test-Taking Strategy
Making Comparisons

At a Glance
Students will learn how to answer questions involving comparisons.

Objectives
- Understand how to make comparisons.
- Refer back to a passage or other information source.
- Read answer choices carefully.
- Eliminate incorrect answer choices.

Reduced Student Pages
Teacher's Guide p. 149

Skills Workbook
For more practice making comparisons, use *Skills Workbook* pages 85–86.

More About
Making Comparisons
Although students are familiar with making comparisons themselves, they often misunderstand what they are expected to do on achievement tests. The comparisons they make in everyday life are within contexts they readily understand. On achievement tests, they may be unfamiliar with the context and thus misunderstand the question and the nature of the comparison.

Answer
Student Edition p. 208
1. C, Both reactions and reflexes protect your body from harm.

Activity
The principal reason students make mistakes on comparison questions is that they have misread a question or an answer choice. For this reason, it is essential that students be encouraged to read questions and answer choices carefully before choosing an answer. Students should pay close attention to keywords that define the comparison, being careful not to choose an answer just because it is a reasonable comparison. The correct answer must correspond directly to the question. Practice this skill by reading sample test questions and answers aloud to the class, then have students choose the correct answers and explain their choices.

If You Have Time...
Strategy Options

Skill Help
Take some time to define *comparison* (finding similarities between two or more things) and *contrast* (finding differences between two or more things). Explain that both types of questions may appear on achievement tests and that a similar process can be used to answer them both. Remind students that the correct answer to a comparison/contrast question should be based on the information given in the test rather than on their own opinion or prior knowledge.

Discussion
Introduce the topic of making comparisons by asking students to give examples of comparisons they make every day. Prompt them to respond to topics such as comparing sports or sports teams, why one type of athletic shoe is better than another, how two cities are alike, and so on. Continue the discussion by projecting an overhead of text that contains a comparison, either explicit or implicit. Have the students identify the comparison and explain what it means.

Test-Taking Strategy
Skipping Difficult Questions

At a Glance
Students will learn how to skip difficult test questions and return to them after answering easier questions.

Objectives
- Recognize difficult questions on tests.
- Decide when to skip questions.
- Answer easier questions first.
- Work methodically.

Reduced Student Pages
Teacher's Guide p. 149

Skills Workbook
For more practice skipping difficult questions, use **Skills Workbook** pages 87–88.

More About
Skipping Difficult Questions
Students typically answer the questions on a test in the order they appear. This tendency can adversely affect the scores of many students, particularly those who lack confidence or read below grade level. These students often spend so much time on difficult items that they don't have time to do easier items that appear later on a test. As a result, the students' abilities are underestimated by the test, and they are more likely to be disappointed and frustrated with their own performances.

Answer
Student Edition p. 210
Question 1 is more difficult than question 2.

Discussion
Assemble a list of practice test questions. Copy the questions onto an overhead and display the pages so they can be used for the basis of class or small group discussions. Ask the students to evaluate the questions and decide which are easier and which are harder. Encourage them to look at the characteristics of the questions such as their length and complexity. In addition, have them explain their own opinions about why a question is easy or difficult. Be sure students understand that there are no right or wrong answers. Encourage students to express their own opinions.

If You Have Time…
Strategy Options

Skill Help
Learning to discriminate between easy and difficult questions is not something that will come easily to students. They will require periodic practice, repeated instruction, and encouragement. This skill should be revisited often.

Activity
Make a practice test by assembling ten questions from old or unused tests. Give each student a copy of the practice test. Set a timer for a short period of time, such as four or five minutes. Tell students they must answer eight of the ten questions before time runs out. When they have finished, ask students to explain how they decided which questions to answer.

Test-Taking Strategy
Using Keywords

At a Glance
Students will learn how to use keywords to answer questions.

Objectives
- Identify keywords in test questions.
- Identify keywords in answer choices.
- Work methodically.
- Refer back to a passage to answer a question.

Reduced Student Pages
Teacher's Guide p. 150

Skills Workbook
For more practice using keywords, use **Skills Workbook** pages 89–90.

More About
Using Keywords
Many test-takers, both children and adults, fail to use one of the most critical aspects of a question: keywords. These words often lead to the right answer to the question or to the part of the passage where the right answer can be found. The two elements involved in using keywords are how to identify them and how to use them.

Answer
Student Edition p. 213
1. D, The earthquake with the same magnitude as the earthquake in Iran

If You Have Time…
Strategy Options

Activity
Have students work together in small groups to practice finding and using keywords. Students should read questions and answer choices aloud, then explain their problem-solving strategy.

Skill Help
Work from the simplest and most obvious keywords to the most subtle keywords. The most obvious keywords are critical words such as *not,* modifiers such as *most important,* and specific terms, names, or dates. One way to get students to attend to these words is to contrast skimming with reading carefully.

Discussion
Provide students with sample test questions taken from test-preparation materials, end of unit tests, or another source. If possible, display some questions using an overhead projector. Go through the questions and help the students identify the keywords and explain what they mean. Lead students in a discussion of how the keywords in questions and answer choices can help identify relevant sections of a passage.

Test-Taking Strategy
Using Context

At a Glance
Students will learn how to use context to derive word or phrase meaning.

Objectives
- Use context to derive word or phrase meaning in test questions.
- Work methodically.
- Refer back to a passage to answer a question.
- Analyze answer choices.

Reduced Student Pages
T*eacher's Guide* p. 150

Skills Workbook
For more practice using context, use ***Skills Workbook*** pages 91–92.

More About
Using Context
Achievement tests often require students to derive word or phrase meaning in a given passage. In some cases, students can use prior knowledge to answer this type of question. In other cases, they must base their answer solely on the context of the passage. This can be difficult for many students, particularly if they are inclined to answer impulsively.

Answer
Student Edition p. 214
1. B, artificial

Discussion
Items involving context are especially perplexing to students who fall prey to "attractive distractors." These are incorrect answer choices that are plausible for one reason or another. With context items, distractors can easily be made attractive by reflecting at least one meaning of the word or phrase or by being logical. A good way to help students avoid this pitfall is to analyze items with them, having them identify why the distractors are wrong given the context of a passage. Find several examples of attractive distractors in sample test questions, then read and discuss them with the class.

If You Have Time...
Strategy Options

Skill Help
With a little instruction, students will understand what it means to use context to define words or phrases. It is a challenge to get students to work methodically and apply what they have learned in the testing situation. When under pressure, many students will simply choose an answer that is the most obvious meaning of the word or phrase, not the one defined by the context. Repeated instruction and practice is the best way to help students avoid this tendency.

Activity
Begin by explaining to students that words and phrases often have various meanings, and that meaning can be defined by the context in which a word is used. The word "ruler," for example, means one thing in mathematics and another in history. Have students use materials they are reading to find words or phrases that are defined by their context.

Test-Taking Strategy
Working Carefully

At a Glance
Students will learn how to avoid making careless mistakes on tests by working carefully.

Objectives
- Read questions carefully.
- Read answer choices carefully.
- Analyze questions and answer choices.
- Refer back to a passage to answer questions.
- Compare answer choices.

Reduced Student Pages
Teacher's Guide p. 151

Skills Workbook
For more practice working carefully, use *Skills Workbook* pages 93–94.

More About
Working Carefully
Students often make the mistake of rushing through test questions, not taking the time to thoroughly read questions and answer choices. In many cases, teachers can identify students who need instruction and practice in working carefully by looking at students' standardized test scores. Underachievers are often students who don't work carefully.

Answer
Student Edition p. 217
1. D, How people are protecting coral reefs

Activity
Display a practice page from a standardized test using an overhead projector. Walk students through the process of answering the questions one step at a time: skimming the passage, skimming the questions to identify the easiest ones, reading questions and answer choices carefully, and so on. Then divide students into small groups and have them repeat the activity with other materials, answering the questions as a group. Repeat this activity several times throughout the year, varying the groups.

If You Have Time...
Strategy Options

Skill Help
Students may have trouble distinguishing between working carefully on a specific project, which they may often do, and working carefully on an achievement test. It is important to address working carefully as a teachable skill, practicing it throughout the year and reviewing it just before testing time.

Discussion
Have students discuss other activities or situations when working carefully is important. For example, when driving a car, when using chemicals such as cleaning supplies, when cooking, or when handling fragile items. Ask students to explain why extra care is needed in these cases and what the results can be of careless actions.

Test-Taking Strategy
Using Logic

At a Glance
Students will learn how to use logic when unsure of an answer or when estimating.

Objectives
- Use given information to make an estimate or informed guess.
- Read questions carefully.
- Compare answer choices.
- Use logic when eliminating answer choices.
- Refer back to a passage, graph, or other information source.

Reduced Student Pages
Teacher's Guide p. 151

Skills Workbook
For more practice using logic, use *Skills Workbook* pages 95–96.

More About
Using Logic
Students are often warned against guessing, yet the best test-takers are often students who can use the process of elimination and logic to guess intelligently when answering test questions. On some tests, there is an adjustment for guessing. Adults use guessing in one form or another every day. Being instructed in using logic to make intelligent guesses will give your students an opportunity to learn this skill systematically.

Answer
Student Edition p. 218
1. C, 225,000 square miles

Discussion
Discuss with students the everyday instances when people must use logic and make guesses. Mention things such as making a turn in an automobile in an unfamiliar area, deciding what to wear when you don't know the weather forecast, choosing a road to take on a busy traffic day, and so on. One of the reasons students are often reluctant to use logic to make a guess is because they think their choice could be wrong. Explaining that using logic is an important thinking skill will help students see the practice as more acceptable.

If You Have Time...
Strategy Options

Activity
Use an overhead projector or board to display some complicated or difficult sample test questions and answer choices. Have students skim the information sources and then answer the questions as a group. Instead of trying to answer the questions traditionally, however, have the students analyze each answer choice to decide which ones are good guesses. Have the students explain the logic they used for each choice.

Skill Help
Explain to students that using logic is not the same as choosing answers at random. Guesses and estimates should be based on information given in a test. Eliminating obviously incorrect answers in order to narrow choices is often a good way to begin the process of using logic.

Teacher Reference

Reduced Student Edition Pages . . . 100

Skills Workbook Answers 153

Skill 1
HOW TO
Make and Use a Model

Shaking in Your Shoes

Imagine that, without any warning, the ground beneath your feet begins to move. It seems like such a long time, but it is only seconds before the shaking stops. In that brief amount of time, buildings, bridges, and roads can collapse or be destroyed.

An **earthquake** is a shaking of the ground caused by the sudden movement of rock below Earth's surface. Stresses within Earth push against underground rocks. When the stress becomes great enough, the rocks snap into a new position, releasing energy. Like ripples in a pond, the energy travels through Earth in waves. As the waves move, Earth's surface can shake, roll, and bend. Many earthquakes form along a fault. A **fault** is a break in Earth's crust where rocks have broken and shifted. During an earthquake the rocks on both sides of a fault can move.

One way to understand what happens during an earthquake is to make a model. A **model** shows what something looks like or how something behaves.

STEPS IN Making and Using a Model

1 Decide What to Show

Think about what you would like to show. Once you decide what to show, write a statement that describes your model. Tell what your model will show and what you hope to learn from building the model. This will help you stay focused as you work on your model.

2 Choose Materials

Decide what to use to make your model. Choose materials to represent different parts or objects. Look for objects that have the same color, shape, or texture as the original. If your model will show movement, look for materials that bend, flow, or move like the original.

3 Put It Together

Gather your materials. Then put the model together and use it to show the process. Add labels to tell the names of important parts or details. You can also include arrows to show movement. Check the statement that you wrote earlier. Make sure that your model shows what you planned to show.

4 Compare and Contrast

As you use your model, compare and contrast your model with the original. Look for similarities and differences between how your model works and the actual process.

EXAMPLE OF Making and Using a Model
Cara made a model to show how rocks move along fault lines. Look below to see what she did.

Purpose

I will build a clay model to show different ways that rock layers move along a fault line. Building the model will help me show what causes an earthquake.

Materials:
- Modeling clay in different colors
- Paper for arrows
- Toothpicks

Each clay block represents the rocky layers of Earth's crust on a separate side of a fault line. By moving my hands forward and back, I model one process of how the rocks slide past each other at a fault line. The model's movement is in the same direction as Earth's real movement. The model does not show the effect of the movement.

Compare and contrast

San Andreas fault in California

USE THIS SKILL
Make and Use a Model

Study the model below. Then answer the questions.

1. What does the water represent?
2. What does the toothpick-structure represent?
3. How could you use this model to show what happens during an earthquake?
4. How is this model like the real thing?
5. How is this model different from the real thing?

TEST TIP — On a test you may be asked to explain a process based on a model. Think about what the model shows. Read the labels. Look for arrows that show movement or the flow of events. Refer to the model to answer each question.

Skill 2
HOW TO
Measure

Using a Thermometer

What happens when you leave a mug of hot chocolate on the table while you go outside to play? Most likely your drink will be cool by the time you come in from outside. Why is that? What happens to the heat?

All matter is made of molecules. Molecules are always moving. The faster the movement, the more energy there is. We notice that energy as heat. As energy moves from warmer objects to cooler ones, you feel heat. When you press your hand against a warm mug, the energy transfers, or moves, from the mug to your fingers. Heat transfers from a warmer substance to a cooler one—in this case the mug is warmer than your skin. Heat also transfers from the hot drink to the air in the room around it. In time your drink will reach the same temperature as the air.

A substance's temperature can provide one sign of heat. **Temperature** shows how warm or cold one thing is compared with another. Scientists use the Celsius temperature scale to measure temperature. We express temperature in degrees Celsius and write it as °C. When you **measure** something, you compare its size or amount to a standard unit. When you measure temperature, you compare the temperature of one substance to the temperatures at which water freezes and boils. At 0 °C, water freezes. Water boils at 100 °C.

A **thermometer** is a tool that measures temperature. Most thermometers are formed from a clear glass or plastic tube filled with liquid. This liquid is usually alcohol, tinted red to make it easy to see. As the liquid in the tube warms, its molecules move more quickly and take up more space. The liquid expands as it warms and moves up the tube. When the liquid cools, the molecules move more slowly

and take up less space. The liquid contracts and moves down the tube.

Once you become familiar with the range of temperatures, you can estimate the temperatures of various substances. A temperature estimate is your best guess of how warm or cool something feels. After you have made your estimate, you can check it by taking a measurement with a thermometer. You can use the steps on the next page to help you measure temperature.

STEPS IN Measuring

1 Choose a Thermometer

You use different kinds of thermometers to measure temperature. If you need to check the temperature of the air outside, you need to use a thermometer that is made for outdoor use. If you need to check your body temperature, you need to use a thermometer that is made for that purpose. If you want to measure the temperature of a liquid, you need a liquid thermometer.

2 Use It Properly

To get an accurate temperature reading, it is important to use the thermometer correctly.

If you are measuring air temperature, place the thermometer off the ground. You can hang the thermometer on a wall. You can also attach a stick to the back of the thermometer and then put the stick in the ground. Be sure to keep the thermometer out of direct sunlight.

To measure the temperature of a liquid, gently lower the thermometer into the liquid. Hold the thermometer so that the bulb, or lower end, is in the middle of the liquid, not touching the sides or bottom of the container. Do not stir with the thermometer.

3 Check the Scale

Before you read a thermometer you should look at the scale. The °C at the end of the thermometer shows what scale the thermometer uses. This thermometer measures temperature in degrees Celsius. Numbers above 0 °C are above freezing. Numbers below 0 °C are below freezing and are written as negative numbers. For example, a temperature of 10 degrees below freezing is expressed as –10 °C. Each line on this thermometer stands for two degrees. Always determine what each line represents before you read the thermometer.

4 Read the Temperature

Once the column of liquid stops moving in the tube, you can read the temperature. As you hold the thermometer, focus on the level of the red liquid. Find the scale line that is closest to the top of the liquid in the tube. Remember to consider what each line represents, such as one degree, two degrees, or five degrees. Then count up or down from the nearest number. The number you end on is the temperature of the substance you are measuring.

TIP Be careful when measuring hot liquids. Both the thermometer and the container that holds the liquid can feel very warm to the touch.

EXAMPLE OF **Measuring**

Nate made a weather station so that he could observe the weather. Read how he measured the air temperature.

Choose a thermometer → Use it properly

Check the scale →
- I attached an outdoor thermometer to a stick. Then I stuck the thermometer in the ground in a shady place in my backyard.
- The scale was in degrees Celsius. Each line on the thermometer stood for two degrees.
- I checked the thermometer a few hours later. I read the temperature. It was 34 °C outside.

Read the thermometer →

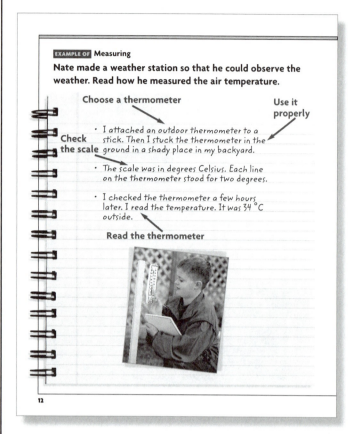

USE THIS SKILL
Measure

Look at the pictures below. Then answer the questions.

Which picture shows how to correctly measure the temperature of a liquid? What is wrong with the other picture?

TEST TIP — You may be asked to do math problems about measurements on a test. Be sure to pay attention to the units of measure when you do your computations. Solve the problem and then compare your results with the answer choices.

Skill 3
HOW TO
Choose the Right Tool

Making a Compost Pile

The average American creates more than two kilograms of trash each day. Much of that waste ends up in landfills—giant land sites where trash is dumped and buried.

Compost pile

Using a compost pile is one way to reduce the amount of waste in landfills. A compost pile can turn leaves, twigs, and grass clippings into compost. **Compost** is a fertile, dirtlike substance that people add to gardens to enrich the soil. Yard wastes are organic, or once-living, materials. Under the right conditions, microorganisms, such as bacteria, will break down the organic matter into nutrient-rich compost.

To build a compost pile you will need some measuring tools. A **tool** is something that helps a person do a job. To measure length, you could use a ruler, a meterstick, or a tape measure. Learning the differences between these measuring tools will help you choose the best tool for the job.

STEPS IN **Choosing the Right Tool**

1 Learn the Process

Think through each step in the process. Identify all the jobs you need to do. Decide what materials you will use. Find how much of each one you will need. Think about what measurements you need to make.

2 Choose the Right Tool

Think about what tools could help you accomplish your tasks. Then narrow your choices. Decide which tool works best for each job.

Tool	What It Measures
Ruler	Use a ruler to measure short lengths. A standard ruler measures up to 30 centimeters. Each centimeter is divided into ten parts. Each part is 1/10 of a centimeter, or 1 millimeter.
Meterstick	Use a meterstick to measure lengths up to 1 meter or 100 centimeters.
Tape measure	Use a tape measure to measure lengths over 1 meter. Centimeter and meter numbers appear on most tape measures. Because most tape measures are flexible, you can use them to measure curved lengths.

EXAMPLE OF Choosing the Right Tool

Read how Kaya chose tools when she built a compost pile.

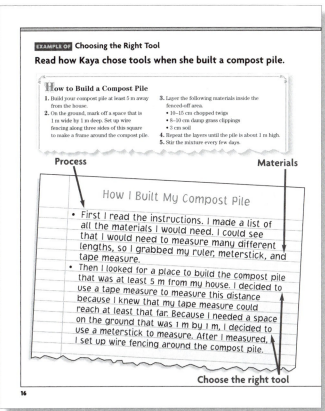

How to Build a Compost Pile
1. Build your compost pile at least 5 m away from the house.
2. On the ground, mark off a space that is 1 m wide by 1 m deep. Set up wire fencing along three sides of this square to make a frame around the compost pile.
3. Layer the following materials inside the fenced-off area.
  • 10–15 cm chopped twigs
  • 8–10 cm damp grass clippings
  • 3 cm soil
4. Repeat the layers until the pile is about 1 m high.
5. Stir the mixture every few days.

Process → ← Materials

How I Built My Compost Pile

- First I read the instructions. I made a list of all the materials I would need. I could see that I would need to measure many different lengths, so I grabbed my ruler, meterstick, and tape measure.
- Then I looked for a place to build the compost pile that was at least 5 m from my house. I decided to use a tape measure to measure this distance because I knew that my tape measure could reach at least that far. Because I needed a space on the ground that was 1 m by 1 m, I decided to use a meterstick to measure. After I measured, I set up wire fencing around the compost pile.

→ Choose the right tool

USE THIS SKILL
Choose the Right Tool

Read each item below. Then write which tool is best for the job—ruler, meterstick, or tape measure.

1. Pour a layer of sand 5 cm thick.
2. Measure the width of your classroom.
3. Measure the circumference of a ball.
4. How long is the goldfish?
5. Find the length of the book.
6. How wide is the front door?
7. What is the distance from one end of the hall to the other?
8. Make a crate that is 1 m high.
9. What is the distance between the houses?
10. How long is your finger?

TEST TIP On a test you may be asked to choose the best tool for an activity. Read the steps in the process. Pay close attention to the details. Think about what the question is asking. Choose the tool that is most useful to complete the activity.

Skill 4
HOW TO
Make a Hypothesis

Magnet Mysteries

Julia attached the note to the refrigerator with a magnet. She tried to attach her art project to the refrigerator, too, but the magnet would not hold the heavy picture on the refrigerator. The picture just fell to the floor.

A **magnet** is an object that attracts iron and some other metals. Since a refrigerator door is built from iron-containing metal, the magnet clings to it.

Magnets do not need to touch iron-containing objects in order to work. The magnet stuck to the refrigerator even though a sheet of paper separated the two. Yet the magnet did not stick when heavier paper separated the magnet and the refrigerator.

Julia wondered what would happen if she tried a larger magnet. She wrote her ideas in a hypothesis. A **hypothesis** is a statement that tries to answer a question about how or why something happens. A hypothesis can also give a prediction about what might happen in an investigation.

STEPS IN Making a Hypothesis

1 Make Observations

A hypothesis must be based on observations. Use your senses to observe the situation. Record your observations. Then review your observations to spot common features or events.

2 Use What You Know

Recall facts and ideas you've read about or learned in school. Think about your own experiences. Think about how these ideas relate to what you observe.

3 Ask Questions

Write questions about what you observe. Make sure your questions can be answered by collecting evidence. Then choose one question as your focus.

4 Make a Hypothesis

Write a hypothesis. The hypothesis should provide an answer to the question you chose. Put your hypothesis into sentence form, using the words *if* and *then*. State your hypothesis so that you can test it.

5 Conduct a Test

Design an experiment to test your hypothesis. Carry out the test. Compare your results with your hypothesis. Don't worry if your hypothesis turns out to be false. A false hypothesis provides valuable information.

← Hypothesis

If a larger magnet is used to attach the heavier paper to the refrigerator, then the magnet will be able to hold the paper to the refrigerator.

EXAMPLE OF Making a Hypothesis

Julia made a hypothesis to predict what would happen if she used a larger magnet to attach her picture to the refrigerator. Look below to see what she did.

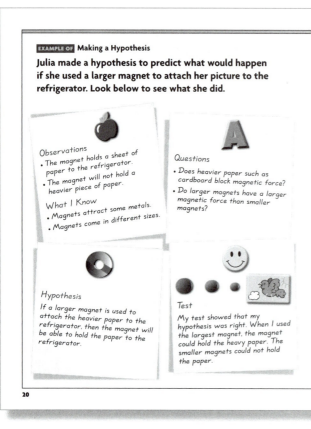

Observations
- The magnet holds a sheet of paper to the refrigerator.
- The magnet will not hold a heavier piece of paper.

What I Know
- Magnets attract some metals.
- Magnets come in different sizes.

Questions
- Does heavier paper such as cardboard block magnetic force?
- Do larger magnets have a larger magnetic force than smaller magnets?

Hypothesis
If a larger magnet is used to attach the heavier paper to the refrigerator, then the magnet will be able to hold the paper to the refrigerator.

Test
My test showed that my hypothesis was right. When I used the largest magnet, the magnet could hold the heavy paper. The smaller magnets could not hold the paper.

USE THIS SKILL
Make a Hypothesis

Read each item below. Write whether each hypothesis is worded correctly or incorrectly. Tell why you think each incorrectly written hypothesis is not correct.

1. Some rocks are naturally magnetic.
2. Can a magnet stick to a corkboard?
3. Can you give magnetic properties to a nail?
4. If the paper clip is plastic, then a magnet will not move it.
5. What happens to iron filings when you pour them over a magnet?
6. A bar magnet has a north-seeking magnetic pole and a south-seeking magnetic pole.
7. If you touch like poles of two magnets together, then the magnets push away from each other.
8. Are some magnets stronger than others?

TEST TIP On a test you may be given a set of data and asked to choose a hypothesis that explains it. Review the data. Don't just choose the hypothesis that makes sense to you. The correct answer tells most about the data.

Skill 5
HOW TO
Collect Data

Think Fast!

Did you know that many professional baseball pitchers throw baseballs that travel at 153 kilometers per hour? That's nearly 50 kilometers per hour faster than a car drives down the highway! In less than four-tenths of a second, the ball soars from the pitcher's mound to home plate. How can a player hit a ball moving at that speed?

Even the best professional players don't successfully hit each time. In fact, if a professional baseball player gets three hits for every ten times at bat, the experts consider the player to be an excellent hitter.

What makes a baseball player successful? One reason is an athlete's superior reaction time. **Reaction time** is the length of time it takes to move after a signal. In this case the signal comes when the player decides to hit the ball. Small visual clues help the player decide how and when to swing. The player's eye sends a message to the brain that controls the muscles. The brain then sends a signal to the muscles, telling the player to swing. Because the ball moves so quickly, there is no time to spare before the player reacts. Too slow of a reaction time means a strike or a missed hit.

Sports fans aren't the only people who collect **data,** or statistics and information, about athletic performance. One reason scientists collect data about reaction time is to find out more about how people learn. Studies show that only by going through the motions over and over do people learn complex skills, such as hitting a fastball. Scientists investigate strategies that help people gain new skills. They study the effects of practice. They even try to determine how long the most effective training sessions last and how frequently practices should be held. Scientific studies such as these can help coaches boost their players' performance.

Scientists collect data by making measurements and recording observations. They record the data in graphs, tables, charts, and diagrams. In order for the data to be meaningful, scientists must collect data from many **trials,** or tests. Think of it this way. Players have good days and bad days. If you measured reaction time only on a bad day, the data would be misleading. Measuring reaction time whenever the player comes to bat provides a much different picture. It takes many trials to get enough data to draw meaningful conclusions.

STEPS IN Collecting Data
Follow these steps to collect data.

1 Make Observations

Make observations as you carry out your investigation. Write everything that happens. Use your senses to observe. Describe details. Add to the observation record each time you conduct more trials.

2 Take Measurements

The nature of the investigation determines the type of measurements you need to take. Measurements might include time, distance, weight, height, heart rate, or pulse. Some measurements are expressed in standard units, such as minutes, meters, and grams. Some measurements are based on a scale.

3 Check for Accuracy

Pay attention to the numbers. Measure carefully. Check the accuracy of the instruments. For instance, if collecting players' weights is part of the investigation, then an accurate scale is a must. Take care as you record the information. It is easy to reverse the numbers or mix up the data you gathered about one test subject with the data you collected from another.

TIP Think of data as the evidence you gather during an investigation. Because the conclusions you draw from your investigation are based on your evidence, the data must be accurate and complete.

4 Display the Data

Choose an appropriate format for recording the data. Draw a diagram to show how something is put together, how something works, or the steps in a process. Use a table to organize numbers into groups. Draw a sketch to show how something looks. Write sentences to explain details or give your impression.

5 Label the Data

Write labels to clearly identify what the data show. Add titles that summarize the content of the data collection. Write captions and draw arrows to explain details and relationships in illustrations.

6 Conduct Repeat Trials

Test results vary. Determine how many trials you need in order to gather enough data. Repeat the tests to collect the data. Record observations and take measurements for each separate trial.

Brian Batter: Hitting Statistics

Year	At Bats	Hits
1987	30	12
1988	435	128
1989	570	181
1990	584	218
1991	562	210
1992	567	212
1993	581	220
1994	619	211
1995	595	210
1996	593	198
1997	575	213
1998	535	176
1999	579	205
2000	569	200
2001	576	170
2002	550	151
2003	557	162

EXAMPLE OF Collecting Data
Read how Maggie collected and recorded data in an investigation about reaction time.

Maggie conducted an investigation to study reaction time to a visual signal. Sam held a ruler near the tip. Susan held her hand near the zero mark at the opposite end of the ruler, ready to grab the ruler when Sam dropped it. Each time Sam dropped the ruler, Maggie measured how far the ruler fell before Susan caught it.

Observations

After each trial, Susan held her hand below the ruler. Sam waited anywhere from 1 to 5 seconds before he dropped the ruler. Since Susan did not know exactly when Sam would drop the ruler, she could not move her hand before she saw the ruler start to fall.

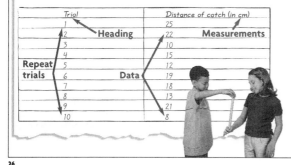

Trial	Distance of catch (in cm)
1	25
2	22
3	10
4	15
5	12
6	19
7	18
8	13
9	21
10	8

(Heading, Measurements, Repeat trials, Data)

USE THIS SKILL
Collect Data

Read the description of the investigation below. Make a table to show the data. Then answer the questions.

Each student held a stopwatch. After the teacher said, "Go," the students quickly clicked their stopwatches on and off. Students recorded the time displayed on their stopwatches. They repeated the test five times. Here are the results of their investigation.

Maria: 0.45 seconds   0.43 seconds   0.44 seconds   0.33 seconds   0.37 seconds
Dan: 0.60 seconds   0.55 seconds   0.45 seconds   0.50 seconds   0.47 seconds
Sally: 0.53 seconds   0.44 seconds   0.37 seconds   0.48 seconds   0.36 seconds
Henry: 0.77 seconds   0.52 seconds   0.57 seconds   0.60 seconds   0.55 seconds
Cho: 0.81 seconds   0.63 seconds   0.71 seconds   0.67 seconds   0.77 seconds
Jamal: 0.58 seconds   0.52 seconds   0.47 seconds   0.43 seconds   0.50 seconds

1. What type of data did the students collect?
2. In what standard units did they report their measurements?

TEST TIP On a test you may be asked to answer questions about data shown in a table. Skim the table. Choose the answer that is best supported by the data.

Skill 6
HOW TO
Control Variables

Changing How Plants Grow

Why do people in some parts of the country mow the lawn twice a week in May but only once during the month of September? This is not a riddle. It is because of the rain. In the warm, wet days of spring, grass grows quickly. By September, when it rains less often, the grass barely grows at all.

Like all living things, plants have needs. Green plants, such as grass, use sunlight to make their own food. They also need water. Different types of plants need different amounts of water. When they don't get enough water, plants grow slowly or not at all.

Suppose you wanted to determine the best growing conditions for grass. You could look at variables that affect the plant's growth. A **variable** is anything that can change the results of an experiment. The amount of water is one variable. The amount of sunlight is another.

STEPS IN Controlling Variables

1 Decide What to Test

Think about what you want to find. If you want to see how sunlight affects the growth of grass, you will change only the amount of sunlight you provide. Everything else about the plants will need to be the same. For example, you should use the same kind of grass plants and give the plants the same amount of water. When doing a test, only one variable at a time should be changed.

2 List Other Variables

Identify the other variables that could change the results of the experiment. Keep these other variables constant, or the same.

3 Do Your Tests

Now do your tests, changing only one variable: sunlight. Include enough plants in your tests to see which grow the most, plants grown in darkness or plants grown in sunlight. Record the results of your tests. Repeat the tests several times to see if your results are similar with each test. Look back at the variable you tested. How did the change affect the results?

TIP Even when you change only one variable and control the others, results can vary from test to test. It is a good idea to use several samples in each test.

EXAMPLE OF Controlling Variables

Thomas wanted to know how the amount of water given to a plant affects how it grows. Look below to see what variables he controlled during his test.

Question: How does the amount of water affect the growth of grass? ← **Variable to test**

Variable to test: Amount of water

Variables to keep the same:
- Type of grass seed
- Time of day grass watered
- Kind of soil
- Size and kind of container
- Amount of sunlight

Plant	Amount of Water (every other day)	Height of Plants (Oct. 1)	Height of Plants (Oct. 7)
A-1	5 mL	6 cm	7 cm
A-2	5 mL	6 cm	6 cm
B-1	30 mL	6 cm	11 cm
B-2	30 mL	6 cm	10 cm

← **Results**

The plants that got 30 mL of water every other day grew much faster than those that got 5 mL of water.

USE THIS SKILL
Control Variables

Look at the picture below. Then answer the questions.

What variable is this student testing? What question do you think she hopes to answer? List at least three other variables she could test. Write a question for each of those variables.

TEST TIP On a test you may be asked to identify the variable that caused the change in an experiment. Remember that only one variable is changed. The other variables stay the same.

Skill 7
HOW TO
Design an Experiment

What Do Seeds Need?

Marwan opened the seed packet. As he scattered the radish seeds in the garden, he wondered how they begin to grow. Would all the seeds grow into radishes?

When you buy a packet of seeds, they are dormant. That means that the seeds will not begin to grow until they are under the right conditions. A dormant seed will begin to grow when it has water, oxygen, and the correct temperature. Not all the seeds in a seed packet will grow. The pictures below show how a bean seed **germinates**, or sprouts.

When the dormant seed has what it needs, it will germinate.

Tiny roots push through the seed coat and begin to grow down.

The top part of the root grows up and becomes the stem.

The young seedling has leaves, a stem, and roots.

To find out more about germinating seeds, Marwan decided to design an experiment. An **experiment** is a scientific test. The goal of an experiment is to gain more information about a problem and test a hypothesis. In an experiment you must consider all the variables that could change the outcome of the experiment. Then you need to control the variables, keeping them all the same, except for the one that you want to test. Marwan started with a hypothesis. Then he identified all the variables that could affect the results of the experiment.

My hypothesis
If groups of seeds receive different amounts of water, then the group with the most water will have more seeds germinate.

Variables to keep the same
- Kind of seeds
- Temperature of seeds
- Amount of light seeds receive
- Materials used

Variable to test
Amount of water

I will put radish seeds into three groups:
1. Seeds without any water
2. Seeds given 50 mL of water
3. Seeds given 150 mL of water

I will observe how many seeds in each group germinate.

STEPS IN Designing an Experiment

1 Write a Plan

After you make a hypothesis and decide what variable you will test, you are ready to design your experiment. Decide how you will carry out the test and write a step-by-step plan. Choose your words carefully so that your directions are clear and easy to follow. Give complete details. Put your steps in the order in which they should be done.

2 Decide How to Record Data

Think about how you will collect and record your data. You can take notes in a notebook. You can take photographs or draw sketches in a journal. If you will need to record measurements or other numbers you might make a table. You can also show your data in a graph.

Observations (How many seeds germinated?)			
Day	Group 1	Group 2	Group 3
1			
2			
3			
4			
5			
6			

3 List Materials and Tools

Identify all the materials you will need. In addition to the actual items that you need to carry out the test, you will also need tools to collect data and make observations. Write a list of all the materials and tools you will use.

Materials
Radish seeds
Seed starter mix
Measuring cup
3 resealable plastic bags
3 plastic cups
Masking tape
Marker
Plastic spoon
Water
Paper

TIP You should also plan to repeat your tests at least a few times. Multiple tests will give you a clearer picture of what is happening in your experiment.

4 Conduct Your Test

Once you have drawn up your plans, you are ready to conduct your test. Perform all the steps. Remember to follow your plan exactly. Follow exactly the same steps each time you repeat the test. Be sure to add data or observations to your notebook or table after each test. Record any numbers neatly and accurately. Later you will analyze your data and observations, drawing conclusions about whether or not the information you recorded supports your hypothesis.

EXAMPLE OF Designing an Experiment

Look below to see how Marwan designed an experiment to test his hypothesis.

My hypothesis
If groups of seeds receive different amounts of water, then more seeds will germinate in the group with the most water.

Plan ← Step-by-step plan
1. Label 3 plastic bags with masking tape and a marker. Use the labels *1, 2,* and *3*.
2. Scoop 150 mL of seed starter mix into the measuring cup. Pour the seed starter mix into a cup. Place 5 radish seeds in the cup and add a thin layer of the mix. Place the cup inside the bag and seal the bag.
3. Repeat step 2 but add 50 mL of water to the seed starter mix before adding the seeds. Mix the water and seed starter mix with a spoon.
4. Repeat step 2 again but add 150 mL of water.
5. Place the bags in the same place so they stay at the same temperature and receive the same amount of light.
6. Observe the seeds each day for ten days. Each day record how many seeds in each group have germinated.

Materials ← Materials and tools
3 resealable plastic bags
Masking tape
Marker
Plastic spoon
Measuring cup
Seed starter mix
3 plastic cups
Radish seeds
Water
Paper

USE THIS SKILL

Design an Experiment

Use the information below to help you design an experiment. Write your plan on another piece of paper.

Hypothesis: If groups of seeds receive different amounts of light, then more seeds will germinate in the group with the most light.

Variable that can change:
Amount of light seeds receive

Variables to keep the same:
- Kind of seeds
- Amount of water
- Temperature
- Materials used

TEST TIP
You may be asked to answer test questions about an experiment. Keep in mind the purpose of an investigation. A good experiment tests a hypothesis. To evaluate the plan, determine whether the experiment provides reliable data. That data should help prove or disprove the hypothesis.

Skill 8
HOW TO
Draw Conclusions

Eugenie Clark Studies Sharks

Dr. Eugenie Clark

For years scientists thought that sharks acted only on instinct, or inborn patterns. Scientists now know that sharks can learn from experience.

Much of what we know about how sharks learn comes from the work of Dr. Eugenie Clark. Dr. Clark is a scientist who studies fish. Because no one knew much about shark feeding patterns, she began studying how much food the sharks at her laboratory ate. She built a feeding platform near the water. From there she dropped fish to the sharks. Soon she noticed that the sharks would come to the edge of the platform and wait for their food. It seemed that the sharks had connected the sight of a human with the food they would get. These observations led to a hypothesis. If sharks could learn that people brought food, then they could be taught other things.

Eugenie Clark planned an experiment to test her hypothesis. She would try to teach a shark to bump its nose on a target to get food. Dr. Clark recorded what she did and observed. Then she studied the data and drew conclusions. A **conclusion** sums up and explains the results of an experiment.

STEPS IN Drawing Conclusions

1 Organize the Data

Gather the records you made during your experiment. Display number data in a table so they are easy to read and interpret. Make graphs to plot changes over time or to show comparisons.

2 Interpret the Information

Study all your data, including measurements, journals, and pictures. Reread all your notes and observations. Did you gather enough evidence so you can draw meaningful conclusions? Think about what the data reveal. Look for patterns or trends. Identify cause-and-effect relationships. Reviewing the data can help you pinpoint areas of change and point to connections between events and behaviors.

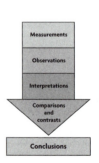

3 Draw Conclusions

Compare the hypothesis with your conclusions. Do the results of the experiment support your hypothesis? What unexpected findings came from the experiment? What new questions did the experiment raise? Write a conclusion statement that sums up the experiment and tells what you learned.

EXAMPLE OF Drawing Conclusions

Read below how Eugenie Clark drew conclusions from her experiment.

Hypothesis

If sharks are rewarded with food, then the sharks will do tricks that they have learned.

- Every day for three months the shark rings a bell on a target to get food.
- Water temperature drops and the shark loses interest in the food and the target.
- Water temperature stays low for ten weeks. The shark does not eat or ring bell during this time.
- Water becomes warmer. For the first time in ten weeks, the shark swims to the target, rings the bell, and gets food.

Observations

The experiment showed that the shark continued to perform the tricks when it was given food. But the shark would not perform the tricks if it was not hungry. The experiment gave two other findings that were not predicted in the hypothesis.

1) Sharks lose interest in eating when the water temperature gets low.
2) Sharks remember what they have learned, even after periods without practice.

Conclusions

USE THIS SKILL
Draw Conclusions

Read the paragraph below. Then write a conclusion statement about the results.

Dr. Clark noticed that the sharks usually swam to the right to get their food. She hypothesized that if she changed the way she fed the sharks, she could get them to turn to the left. She designed an experiment to test her hypothesis. After pressing the target, the shark turned to the right to swim toward its food reward. After ten seconds Dr. Clark took the shark's food out of the water before the shark got there. The shark lost its food. The shark lost its food three times in the same way. On the fourth try, the shark turned to the left and got to the food in less than ten seconds. The shark ate the food.

Lemon shark

TEST TIP A test question may ask you to draw conclusions from a reading passage. Remember that conclusions are based on evidence. Choose the conclusion that makes the most sense when compared with the information in the passage.

Skill 9
HOW TO
Prepare an Observation Report

Curious about Mold

Do you know why adults tell children not to leave leftover food and dirty dishes sitting around? Is it that parents want you to clean up after yourself? That could be one reason. Keeping away uninvited organisms, such as mold, could be another!

Blue cheese, named for its bluish streaks of mold

Mold is a type of fungus. Fungi are among the most common organisms on Earth. Unlike plants that make their own food, fungi live on organic matter. Organic matter comes from once-living organisms. Mold can live on the nutrients found in bread, fruits, and many other foods that people eat. Mold can spoil food. Yet some molds are very useful. Certain cheeses get their flavor from the mold that grows in them. Many beneficial drugs, such as penicillin, come from molds.

A fungus such as mold does not produce seeds. Instead it reproduces by releasing tiny spores into the air. When the spores land in a place with the right conditions, they can begin to grow.

Jeremy loved his grandmother's homemade bread. The only trouble was, if the family didn't eat it soon enough, mold formed on the bread and spoiled it. Jeremy wanted to find out if mold grew better on some foods than others. He decided to test two types of bread—one made with preservatives and one made without preservatives. He photographed the bread each day to show what it looked like. He took notes to help him remember what he saw.

Later he prepared an **observation report.** An observation report is a good way to summarize an investigation. It

Mold on bread

tells what you observed through one or more senses. It explains why you made your observations and what you hoped to find out. It describes the steps you followed and explains what conclusions you drew from your observations. You can use the steps on the next page to help you prepare an observation report for a science investigation or project.

STEPS IN Preparing an Observation Report

1 Make Observations

Gather information for your report by making observations. Use as many senses as are safe and practical to tell what you see, hear, smell, taste, or feel. Record everything you observe. Take measurements. Use a table, graphic organizer, or journal to take notes. Take photographs or draw pictures of what you see.

2 Write Your Purpose

Once you finish your observations, you are ready to start your observation report. Begin by writing your purpose.

The purpose should tell why you carried out the investigation. Explain what questions you tried to answer or the problem you hoped to solve by carrying out the investigation. Limit the purpose statement to one or two sentences.

3 Describe Your Procedure

Describe the procedure you followed. Answer the questions What? How? Where? and When? Explain the steps you followed and tell how you made observations. Include dates and times and tell what measurements you made. Put the steps in order. Keep your explanation simple, but make it clear. Name the materials you used, including specific amounts. List the tools you used as well.

Date	Bread without Preservatives	Bread with Preservatives
April 11	no signs of mold	no signs of mold
April 12	no signs of mold	no signs of mold
April 13	Tiny black spots in center	no signs of mold

4 Describe Your Observations

Gather and organize the notes, pictures, and tables you made as you observed. Expand on these notes as you describe your observations. Write in complete sentences. Explain your observations in the order in which you made them.

The mold was mostly black, but in some areas it was fuzzy and white.

5 Write Your Conclusions

Summarize your results. Explain the key points of what you learned. Tell whether the activity answered your questions or solved the problem you identified at the beginning. Include any unanswered questions or ideas for new observations that you would like to make.

6 Revise and Edit

Reread your observation report. Check that you included each part of the report: Purpose, Procedure, Observations, and Conclusions. Make sure that you presented your ideas in an order that makes sense. Ask yourself if you included enough detail. Revise your work to fix any problems you find. Check punctuation, grammar, and spelling. Pay special attention to capitalization and spelling of scientific words. Correct any errors and make a final, neat copy of your report.

EXAMPLE OF Preparing an Observation Report

As you read the observation report about bread mold, notice how it is organized.

Bread Mold

Purpose: I wanted to learn why mold forms so quickly on my Grandma's homemade bread. I decided to find out if mold grows more quickly on bread without preservatives than on bread with preservatives.

Procedure: I started on April 11. I put one slice of bread with preservatives on a plate labeled P. I put one slice of bread without preservatives on a plate labeled NP. The next day I put each slice of bread into a plastic bag. I labeled the bags. Each day for seven days I used a hand lens to observe the bread. I took pictures of what I saw.

Observations: Neither piece of bread had any signs of mold on the first or second day. On the third day, I did not see any mold on either slice, until I looked with a hand lens. Then I saw tiny black dots on the bread without preservatives. By the fourth day I could see the mold on that slice without using the hand lens. Each day there was more mold. The mold was mostly black, but in some areas it was fuzzy and white. On the sixth day I saw a few tiny spots of mold on the bread with preservatives. By the seventh day there was a bit more mold but still not nearly as much as on the bread without preservatives.

Conclusions: My investigation answered my question about my Grandma's bread. Mold grows more quickly on bread without preservatives than on bread with preservatives. I wonder if keeping Grandma's bread in the refrigerator might help keep mold from growing on it.

USE THIS SKILL

Prepare an Observation Report

Jeremy decided to continue his investigation to figure out how to keep mold from growing on his grandma's bread. Use his notes shown below to write an observation report.

Date	Grandma's Bread in Refrigerator	Grandma's Bread NOT in refrigerator
April 20	No signs of mold	No signs of mold
April 21	No signs of mold	No signs of mold
April 22	No signs of mold	Tiny black specks in center of bread (used hand lens)
April 23	No signs of mold	Can see black spots (without hand lens)
April 24	No signs of mold	Black mold covers about half the slice of bread
April 25	Tiny black spots in center of bread (used hand lens)	Fuzzy white mold begins to form on top of black mold
April 26	Can see a few small black spots in center of bread (without hand lens)	Three fourths of the slice of bread is covered by white fuzz

TEST TIP On a test you may be asked to write a paragraph that describes something you experienced. Begin your paragraph with a topic sentence. Include details and colorful language.

Skill 10
HOW TO Classify

Machines Make Work Easier

How many machines have you used today?

A machine is anything that makes work easier. There are many examples of **simple machines,** and they have some things in common. They have few moving parts and they do not need electricity to work. Simple machines can be used with other machines, or they can be used alone. Scientists classify simple machines into groups. Look at the table that describes the six groups of simple machines. To **classify** means to put things into groups.

Simple Machines	Description
Lever	A lever is an arm that turns around a point. Some levers are used to pull and pry up objects.
Wheel and axle	A wheel and axle is a machine with a wheel that turns around a post. A wheel and axle is a lever that can turn all the way around.
Pulley	A pulley is a rope that is placed over a grooved wheel. Most of the time pulleys are used to lift objects.
Inclined plane	An inclined plane is a flat surface that is higher at one end. Using an inclined plane makes it easier to slide a load upwards than to lift it directly.
Wedge	A wedge is an inclined plane that is used to push objects apart.
Screw	A screw is an inclined plane that winds around a rod into a spiral. Screws are used to hold objects together.

STEPS IN Classifying

1 Study the Information
Look at the information you have. Think about how the items are alike and different.

TIP Keep in mind that items can usually be classified in many different ways.

2 Sort into Groups
Choose one feature that some of the items share but others do not. Place items that share the feature you chose into one group. Place those that do not belong into another group or groups based on other features. Give each group a name that describes the group.

3 Record the Information
Keep track of your classification by making lists, graphic organizers, or charts. These will help make the information you have classified easy to understand.

Simple Machines    **Other Machines**

EXAMPLE OF Classifying

Mrs. Miranda gave each group of students a box of simple machines. See how one group classified the machines.

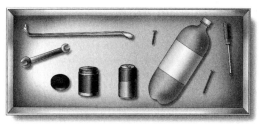

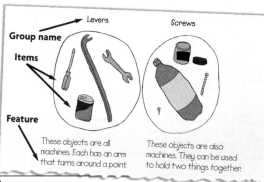

Group name → Levers, Screws
Items →
Feature → These objects are all machines. Each has an arm that turns around a point. / These objects are also machines. They can be used to hold two things together.

USE THIS SKILL
Classify

Look at the simple machines below. Classify the machines into two groups.

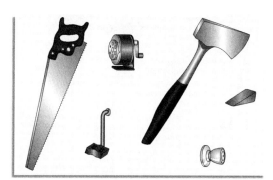

TEST TIP Some tests may ask you to find a word that does not belong in a group. Look for something that is shared by most of the words. Eliminate the one that does not share that thing.

Skill 11
HOW TO
Compare and Contrast

Comparing the Planets

The sun is at the center of the solar system. Around the sun are nine planets.

These planets are put into two groups according to their distance from the sun. The inner planets are Mercury, Venus, Earth, and Mars. The outer planets are Jupiter, Saturn, Uranus, Neptune, and Pluto. The planets have much in common, but the inner planets also differ from the outer planets in many ways. Comparing and contrasting topics like these will help you better understand what you read. To **compare,** think about how two topics are alike. To **contrast,** think about how the topics are different.

STEPS IN Comparing and Contrasting

1 Identify the Topics

Read the paragraph. Decide what two topics the paragraph compares and contrasts.

2 Look for Signal Words

Words that compare: *both, share, like, too, also, all*

The planets <u>all</u> revolve, or move, around the sun.

Words that contrast: *whereas, but, however, more, less*

<u>Whereas</u> *the inner planets are made mostly of rock, the outer planets are made mostly of gases.*

Endings on words, such as *–er* and *–est,* also signal contrast:

The inner planets are <u>warmer</u> than the outer planets.

3 Make a Chart

It may help to write comparisons and contrasts in a chart.

Inner Planets and Outer Planets

Alike	Different
Part of the same solar system	Inner planets are warmer
All are spheres	Most outer planets are larger
Revolve around the sun	Inner planets made of rock; outer planets made of gases
Rotate on an axis	Outer planets are farther from the sun

EXAMPLE OF Comparing and Contrasting

Read the paragraph below that compares and contrasts Venus with Earth. Then look at the chart that shows how the two planets are alike and different.

Signal words

Venus and Earth

Venus is the planet **closest** to Earth. It is sometimes called Earth's twin, because the two planets are close in size. Like Earth, Venus has molten rock at its center. **Both** planets also have mountains and volcanoes. **Unlike** Earth, Venus is always cloudy because its atmosphere is so thick. It takes Venus only seven and a half Earth months to revolve around the sun. Yet Venus rotates so slowly on its axis that a day on Venus is longer than its year! This unusual planet rotates clockwise, the **opposite** direction from Earth's rotation.

Earth and Venus

Alike	Different
They are similar in size	Venus is always cloudy
Both have molten rock in center	Venus revolves around the sun faster than Earth
Both have mountains and volcanoes	Venus rotates more slowly on its axis than Earth
	Venus rotates in the opposite direction from Earth

USE THIS SKILL
Compare and Contrast

Read the paragraph below. Then make a chart to compare and contrast Mars and Earth.

Mars and Earth

As inner planets, Earth and Mars are made mostly of rocks. Instead of the green vegetation of Earth, you would see mostly reddish rocks and dust on Mars. That's because life as we know it on Earth does not exist on Mars. You would not find any lakes or oceans, because Mars is so cold that any water on it is frozen. If you travel to Mars, be sure to take your own air. That's because the atmosphere on Mars is mostly carbon dioxide, not nitrogen and oxygen as we have here on Earth. A day on Mars is about the same length as a day on Earth. It would take fewer days to explore Mars than Earth, though, because Mars is about half the size of Earth. A year on Mars is almost two years on Earth. Be prepared to see not one but two moons in the night sky on Mars.

TEST TIP When taking a test, you might be asked questions about a passage that compares and contrasts two topics. Read the question carefully to learn if you should compare or contrast.

Skill 12
HOW TO
Determine Cause and Effect

Fire!

The firefighter sifts through the charred rubble, looking for clues. Finally the firefighter finds the remains of a campfire left unattended. This clue helps the firefighter figure out what caused the fire that destroyed many acres of forest.

The **cause** is the reason something happens. What happens as a result of the cause is the **effect**. Look for causes and effects in the following reading.

Fires start when a fuel reacts with heat and oxygen. These elements make up the fire triangle. If one of these elements is missing, a fire will not burn. Many wildfires are caused by heat from lightning strikes or unattended campfires. The heat reacts with oxygen in air and a fuel such as wood or pine needles. Firefighters smother wildfires with water so that the fires will stop. The fires go out because one part of the fire triangle is removed.

Use the steps on the next page to help you determine cause and effect.

CAUSE → **EFFECT**

Firefighters smother wildfires with water. → The fires will stop.

STEPS IN Determining Cause and Effect

1 Find Clue Words

Clue words may help you find causes and effects.

Clue words such as *because*, *since*, and *caused by* may signal a cause.

Many wildfires are caused by *heat from lightning strikes or unattended campfires.*

Clue words such as *therefore*, *as a result*, and *so* may signal an effect.

Firefighters smother wildfires with water so that *the fires will stop.*

CAUSE — Heat + Oxygen + Fuel → **EFFECT** — Fire

2 Look for Causes and Effects

Find what happens. This is the effect. Then find why it happens. This is the cause.

What happens? (effect)

The fires go out.

Why does it happen? (cause)

Because one part of the fire triangle is removed

TIP A cause happens before an effect. However, in a sentence, sometimes an effect is written first, followed by its cause.

EXAMPLE OF Determining Cause and Effect

Read the passage below. Think about the relationship between causes and effects.

Fighting Wildfires

Crews of firefighters work together to put out wildfires. **[Cause]** Hand crews of about 20 firefighters create a fire line around a wildfire **so** that the wildfire does not spread to other areas. **[Effect]** A fire line is a strip of land that looks like a trail or small road. Firefighters use axes, chainsaws, and other tools to clear the fire line of brush, trees, and other plants. **[Cause]** **Since** these fuels are removed, the fire will often not spread beyond the fire line. **[Effect]** Sometimes firefighters start small fires to remove plants from the land. **[Effect]** This kind of controlled burn is done **because** firefighters want to remove any fuels in the path of a fire or to prevent a fire from starting in the future. **[Cause]** Removing the fuel from a wildfire is one way to stop it from burning.

USE THIS SKILL
Determine Cause and Effect

Read the paragraph below. Find at least three examples of cause-and-effect relationships.

Controlling Home Fires

Many home fires are caused by people who become careless while cooking. A key to stopping these fires is removing one or more parts of the fire triangle. Small grease fires can be smothered using baking soda. The baking soda forms carbon dioxide as it mixes with liquids in burning foods. The fire goes out because carbon dioxide keeps oxygen from reaching the fuel or burning food. Putting a lid on a burning pot is another way to smother a fire. The lid stops the flow of air to the fire so that the fire does not have oxygen to keep burning. Throwing a bucketful of water on a paper fire may stop it because the water smothers the fire, but water should never be thrown on a grease or electrical fire. It will make these fires worse. A fire extinguisher may help during a home fire if it is used properly. When any fire seems out of control, it is safest to leave the building and call the fire department.

TEST TIP On a test you may be asked to find causes and effects in a reading passage. Read the passage carefully to see if you can find a cause or an effect. Remember that a cause comes before an effect and makes the effect happen.

Skill 13
HOW TO
Tell Fact from Opinion

Coral Reefs

Are coral reefs important to our planet's health? Do they provide a home for many kinds of fish and other animals? Do they take hundreds of years to form? Are they in trouble? The answer to these questions is *yes*.

A **coral reef** looks like it is made of rock, but it is not. A coral reef is made by tiny animals called corals. Colonies, or groups, of corals create a coral reef. Corals produce a hard substance called limestone that acts as a skeleton to protect their soft bodies. When coral colonies die, their limestone skeletons remain. Other coral colonies attach themselves to these skeletons. Over many, many years, a reef forms.

When you read about topics in science, such as coral reefs, you learn facts about people, places, and events. A **fact** tells something that is known to be true, or something that really happened. It is a statement that can be checked. Learning how to find the facts in what you read will help you understand and remember it. Look for facts in the paragraph below.

Coral reefs develop in shallow tropical and subtropical ocean waters. The largest, the Great Barrier Reef, which is located off the coast of northeastern Australia, is more than 1,250 miles long. There is another large coral reef in the Indian Ocean off the east coast of Africa. Some of the other locations of coral reefs are the Caribbean Sea and the waters off the coasts of Indonesia and the Philippines.

Fact: The largest coral reef, the Great Barrier Reef, which is located off the coast of northeastern Australia, is more than 1,250 miles long.

Fact: There is another large coral reef in the Indian Ocean off the east coast of Africa.

STEPS IN Telling Fact from Opinion

When you read about topics in science, you may also read people's opinions. An **opinion** is a statement about what someone feels or believes. You can't prove or check an opinion. Below are some opinions about coral reefs. Notice how the opinions are different from the facts.

"I think coral reefs should be off-limits to boaters and divers. People in boats are always dragging anchors across the reefs. Most divers exploring the reefs break off pieces of coral. These activities make the water so cloudy that it has a bad effect on the whole ecosystem."

Opinion: "I think coral reefs should be off-limits to boaters and divers."

Opinion: "Most divers exploring the reefs break off pieces of coral."

Use these steps to help you tell fact from opinion.

1 Look for Facts

- The names of people or places can sometimes help you find facts.

Some of the other locations of coral reefs are the Caribbean Sea and the waters off the coasts of Indonesia and the Philippines.

- Facts may tell about the size or amount of something. Look for numbers to help find these facts.

. . . the Great Barrier Reef . . . is more than 1,250 miles long.

- Make sure the fact can be checked.

Coral reefs develop in shallow tropical and subtropical ocean waters. Yes, you can do research to see if this fact is correct.

2 Look for Opinions

Remember that opinions cannot be proven true or false. Opinions are a person's beliefs or feelings.

There are certain words that provide clues that a statement may be an opinion. Watch for clue words such as *good, better, best, think, believe, wonderful, bad, worst, terrible, seems, should, more,* and *most*.

"Most divers exploring the reefs break off pieces of coral."

"These activities make the water so cloudy that it has a bad effect on the whole ecosystem."

3 Compare and Contrast

Paragraphs that you read may have both facts and opinions. It may help to list the facts and opinions in a chart.

Facts	Opinions
Many different kinds of sharks live around the Great Barrier Reef.	Sharks are the most dangerous animals around the Great Barrier Reef.
Coral reefs take thousands of years to develop.	Divers shouldn't touch or stand on coral.
Coral can be used to make jewelry.	I think coral jewelry is beautiful.

EXAMPLE OF Telling Fact from Opinion

Read the passage below about coral reefs. Think about facts and opinions as you read.

Coral Reefs

Opinion → Coral reefs are wonderful places. While they take up a very small amount of Earth's surface, they contain a higher number of different kinds of plants and animals than anywhere else in the ocean. Of all ocean species that we have so far identified, 25 percent of them live in and around coral reefs. The only places on Earth that have a higher number of kinds of plants and animals are the tropical rain forests. In addition to the corals themselves, many other animals live in and around the reef. They include shrimp, octopuses, eels, worms, sponges, sea snakes, sea turtles, clams, crabs, lobsters, and sharks, as well as many other kinds of fish. ← Facts

Opinion → As people learn more about coral reefs, they should better appreciate these beautiful places.

USE THIS SKILL
Tell Fact from Opinion

Read the paragraph below. Find one fact and one opinion.

Coral Reefs in Danger

The damage being done to coral reefs around the world is terrible. Storms can bury a reef under sand. When this happens, the corals die. Over the past 20 years, the water temperature has risen. If the water gets too warm, the corals die. Disease is also killing the corals. For example, sea-fan coral in the Caribbean Sea is being killed by a type of fungus.

Humans are part of the problem, as well. Chemical pollution from herbicides and oil drilling has poisoned the water in many areas. Divers and boaters continue to disturb and damage the reefs. If these reefs are allowed to die, people who live near them will lose one of their main sources of food. Finding ways to protect the coral reefs should be one of the world's priorities.

TEST TIP On some tests you may be asked to tell whether a statement is a fact or an opinion. As you read each statement, ask yourself if you could prove it true or false. If the information cannot be checked, it is an opinion.

Skill 14
HOW TO
Find the Main Idea

Nature's Recyclers

The cycle of life on Earth depends on a group of organisms that we do not think about very often. Some of them are so small you cannot see them without a microscope. They are called decomposers. **Decomposers** get their food by breaking down dead organisms into simpler substances. These substances are then returned to the air and soil to be used by other organisms.

When you read about science topics, you need to pick out the main ideas. A **main idea** tells what a paragraph is about. The sentence that contains the main idea is called the **topic sentence**.

The other sentences are called **detail sentences**. They tell more about the main idea.

Often the topic sentence is the first sentence of the paragraph, but it can also be another sentence in the paragraph. In the paragraph that follows, the topic sentence is first.

Decomposers replace chemicals in the soil to keep it rich and fertile. In the fall the leaves of many trees fall off. Decomposers break down the chemicals in the leaves and return them to the soil. They do the same thing to all dead plants and animals. Chemicals from dead plants and animals are returned to the soil.

STEPS IN Finding the Main Idea

Use these steps to find the main idea when you read.

1 Read the Paragraph
Read the paragraph. Watch for words or ideas that appear in more than one sentence.

2 Identify the Topic
Think about what you have read. If you had to tell in a few words what the whole paragraph is about, what would you say? Those few words are the topic.

3 Find the Topic Sentence
Now look for the sentence that best tells about the topic. Remember, to contain the main idea, the sentence must tell what the paragraph is mostly about.

4 Check the Detail Sentences
Once you have chosen the sentence with the main idea, check the other sentences. Each one should tell more about the topic sentence you have chosen.

EXAMPLE OF Finding the Main Idea

Read the following paragraph. Notice the topic sentence that contains the main idea and the detail sentences.

Decomposers

Have you ever left fruit in the refrigerator too long and found something "growing" on it? That something was mold. It was breaking down the fruit into a simpler form. Have you ever seen a tree stump with mushrooms growing on it? They were getting food from the tree stump, but they were also breaking down the wood into a simpler substance that can be absorbed by the soil. Have you ever seen a compost pile in a garden? In it you can be sure that there were millions of bacteria busily breaking down the dead plants into a form that the gardener can use for fertilizer. **Decomposers such as molds, mushrooms, and bacteria are everywhere, working away to recycle dead organisms.**

Detail sentences ← paragraph body
Topic sentence ← last sentence
Main idea ← last sentence

USE THIS SKILL
Find the Main Idea

Read the paragraph below. Find the main idea.

Bacteria

Some forms of bacteria can change dangerous chemicals into harmless ones. Substances from oil spills have endangered the oceans and the organisms that live in them. Scientists have used bacteria to change these substances into ones that are not harmful to living things. Substances used in dry cleaning and antifreeze can be very poisonous to humans. Scientists have found bacteria that remove the poison. What is left is less harmful to the environment.

TEST TIP On some tests you may be asked to identify the main idea in a passage. Read the passage carefully. Then read all the answer choices. Choose the one that best tells about the whole passage. Do not choose an answer that is just a detail from the paragraph.

Skill 15
HOW TO Take Notes

Alternative Fuel-Powered Vehicles

Did you know that some people "plug in" their cars in order to fuel them with electricity? Electric cars are just one kind of alternative fuel-powered vehicle (or AFV) being produced by automobile manufacturers.

An **alternative fuel** is an energy source other than gasoline used to power vehicles such as cars, buses, and motorcycles. Today's alternative energy sources for cars include electricity, natural gas, solar energy, hydrogen, and ethanol made from corn, soybeans, or other plant materials. The automobile

Electric car

industry is producing AFVs to help reduce air pollution and conserve fossil fuels such as oil.

To learn more about alternatives to traditional cars, you can research the latest news about AFVs. You can take notes to help you remember what you read. **Taking notes** is writing important facts about a topic while reading, listening, or watching. You can use the steps on the next page to help you take notes.

STEPS IN Taking Notes

1 Gather Information

Use sources with current information. Look for books and articles with recent publication dates. Other sources of information are encyclopedias, newspapers, informational videos, interviews, and the Internet. Look for answers to the questions Who, What, When, Where, Why, and How in the sources you find. Then find the answers to any other questions you have about your topic.

TIP Choose Internet sources carefully. Information provided by government or education agencies will usually be more accurate than information from other sources.

Make a concept web.
A **concept web** is a way to take notes using ovals connected by lines. To make a web, place your topic in an oval in the center of your paper. Write information about the topic in ovals around the center oval. Connect the ovals with lines.

2 Organize Your Information

You can organize your information in many ways. Here are a few ideas.

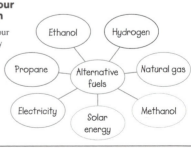

Use index cards.
Index cards are a useful way to keep and organize notes. Write one main idea and its supporting details on each card. Write the name and page numbers of the sources you use on each index card. Arrange the cards in any order you like. You can quickly flip through the cards to find the notes you need.

Cars can use solar energy
- *Some electric cars use solar energy.*
- *Solar cars use photovoltaic cells that collect solar energy.*
- *Solar cars are mostly used in races.*

Seely, Elaine. Solar Cars. Best Book Publishers, 2003, p. 11

Make a gathering grid.
A **gathering grid** is a chart you can use to record information. To make a gathering grid, draw a grid like the one below. Write your topic and the kinds of sources you found across the top. Write your questions in the left column and your answers in the columns to the right. Write the name of the source and the page number where you found the information within each answer box.

Alternative Fuel-Powered Vehicles	Magazines	Books	Internet
Why are they a good idea?	Electric cars use less fossil fuels than traditional cars.	Hydrogen-powered cars cause less pollution than traditional cars.	Hybrid electric cars get more miles per gallon of gas than traditional cars.
	Modern Driver May 2001, p. 58	Cars for a Healthy Planet, p. 10	www.hybrid/information.gov

3 Write the Information

As you gather information through reading, listening, and watching, think about what you want to remember. Take clear notes that you will be able to read and understand later. Write in your own words. Include only the most important information and keep your notes short. You do not have to write in complete sentences. Use keywords, phrases, symbols, and abbreviations.

Ethanol = fuel made from corn, soybeans, & other plants

Hybrid electric vehicle (HEV)

Be sure to record where you found the information. Include the title of the source, author, date of publication, and page number.

Elliott, Jack. Future Cars. AFV Publishing Co., 2002. p. 65

Sometimes you may want to write a quote. A **quote** is the exact words that someone has said or written. When writing a quote, make sure to use quotation marks. Tell who said or wrote the quote and spell the person's name correctly.

"My new HEV gets almost 50 miles per gallon of gas. That's a lot better than my old car. I can go just as fast as I did before too."
—Rita Hernandez

EXAMPLE OF Taking Notes

Look at the notes that one student wrote about the paragraph below.

Electric cars

Electric cars store energy in large batteries that produce the electrical energy to power the car. When the batteries run low, the car's recharger must be plugged into a special outside electrical outlet. Most electric cars can be driven about 100 miles before they need to be recharged. This makes electric cars a practical transportation choice for people who drive only short distances.

Short notes

Electric Cars
- *Store energy in large batteries*
- *The batteries produce electr. energy 2 power the car.*
- *Car must be plugged in 2 recharge when batteries run low*
- *Can drive most electr. cars about 100 mi. before they need 2 be recharged*

Fry, Michelle. "Cars Get Electric." Car News, Inc., 2002, p. 8

Source

USE THIS SKILL

Take Notes

Take notes on the paragraph below.

Hybrid Electric Vehicles

Many drivers who are concerned about air pollution and conserving fossil fuels are becoming interested in hybrid electric vehicles (HEVs). Hybrid electric vehicles combine a small gasoline engine with a battery and an electric motor. HEVs work in many different ways. Sometimes the gasoline engine charges batteries to run the electric motor. The electricity in turn is used to power the car's wheels. Other HEVs are powered by switching back and forth between the gasoline engine and the electric motor, depending on driving conditions. HEVs have many advantages. They produce less harmful emissions and pollution. HEVs also get more miles per gallon of gas than traditional cars.

TEST TIP Some tests may ask you to choose the best summary of a reading passage. Be sure to choose the one that includes the most important ideas of the passage.

Skill 16
HOW TO
Estimate

One Serving, Please

Eating too little or too much is not good for your health. How do you know if you are getting the right servings? You can measure, or you can estimate.

To **estimate** means to get an idea of how big something is or how many of something there are without actually measuring or counting. Use the steps that follow to help you estimate serving sizes.

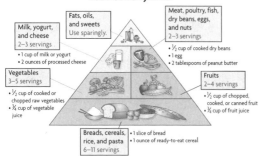

Food Guide Pyramid

STEPS IN Estimating

1 Compare with Real Objects

Imagine the object you are estimating next to an object with which you are more familiar. Compare the sizes.

2 Make Your Estimate

Decide if the object you are estimating is smaller, larger, or about the same size as the object with which you are familiar. You can make your estimate based on this.

3 Check Your Estimate

You should check your estimates occasionally to make sure you are on track. You can measure to be sure you are estimating close to actual serving sizes.

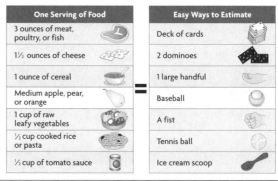

EXAMPLE OF Estimating

Read how one person estimated serving sizes for a food log.

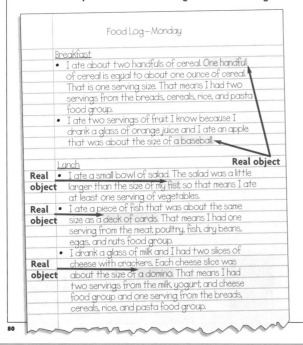

USE THIS SKILL

Estimate

Keep a food log for one day. Estimate and write how many servings from each food group you eat. You can use the Food Guide Pyramid on page 78 and the chart on page 79 to help you. Then answer the questions below.

1. From which food groups do you need to eat more servings?

2. From which food groups do you need to eat less servings?

3. How could you improve your diet?

TEST TIP You may be asked to estimate an amount on a test. Remember that an estimate is not an exact answer. It is a good guess.

Skill 17
HOW TO
Predict

Moving and Changing

Grace put the finishing touches on her sand castle and stood back to admire her work. Soon she felt the waves lapping against her ankles. Grace worried that she built her sand castle too close to the water's edge.

Grace remembered that at different times of the day the waves come up higher on the shore. She knew that water could wash away sand. Grace predicted that the waves would wash away her sand castle. To **predict** means to tell what you think will happen in the future. A prediction is not a guess. It is based on what you observe and what you have learned or experienced.

Scientists study coastlines, fields, and other landscapes to observe the effects of erosion. **Erosion** occurs when particles of rock, sand, or dust are moved. Erosion is caused by five natural forces: gravity, glaciers, wind, running water, and waves. These forces are constantly moving and dropping loose, weathered materials. Because erosion can cause great damage, scientists study the land, make predictions, and try to lessen erosion's effects.

STEPS IN Predicting

Use these steps to help you make predictions.

1 Make Observations

Look closely at what is happening around you. Pay special attention to events and situations that cause you to ask questions.

2 Use What You Know

Think about what you already know about the situation. This could be information you read in a book or learned in school. It could be information you know because of something you experienced or observed in the past.

3 Make a Prediction

Combine what you observed with what you already know about the situation to tell what you think will happen in the future.

> Observations
> My sand castle is near the water's edge.
>
> What I Know
> At different times of the day the waves come up higher on the beach. Other sand castles I have built have been washed away by the waves that hit the sand.
>
> Prediction
> The waves will soon hit my sand castle and wash it away.

EXAMPLE OF Predicting

Look at how one student predicted what will happen in the picture.

> Observations
> A house is built on a beach. The sand around it seems to have eroded.
>
> What I Know
> I have read that coastlines are battered by waves and high winds. This can cause the sand to erode.
>
> Prediction
> The sand around the house will erode even more and the house may fall over.

USE THIS SKILL
Predict

Study the picture of the rock. Write a prediction that tells what will happen to the rock. Tell how you made your prediction.

TEST TIP
On a test you may be asked to read a passage and answer questions about it. Skim the passage and the questions. Answer any questions you think are easy. Then go back and do the harder items.

Skill 18
HOW TO
Infer

Leaves of Three, Let Them Be

Todd ran to get the ball that had rolled into the bushes along the fence. After soccer practice, Todd began to itch. That night he noticed a bumpy, red rash on his arms. He did not know what caused the rash.

Todd knew that the rash looked just like one he got last summer when he accidentally touched some poison ivy. Todd decided that the bushes at the soccer field must have had poison ivy growing around them.

Todd didn't know exactly what caused the rash. He used what he observed and what he knew about poison ivy to **infer**, or explain what happened. You infer all the time. Anytime you use what you have learned or know to explain something that happened, you are inferring. You can use the steps on the next page to help you infer.

I ran into the bushes to get the soccer ball. Now I itch, and I have a bumpy, red rash.
Observations

+

Last year I had a rash that looked just like this. I got it from touching poison ivy.
What you know

=

The bushes must have had poison ivy growing around them. I touched the poison ivy when I got the ball.
Inference

STEPS IN Inferring

1 Make an Observation

You make observations all the time. Your senses help you find out about the world. You can use what you see, hear, smell, taste, or touch to explain events or situations.

I <u>saw</u> a green vine with three leaves.

It had round, green berries growing on the stem.

2 Think about What You Know

After you observe a situation, think about what you know. You might remember information you learned in school, read about in a book, or you might remember something you did or saw before. This information can help you explain what you observed.

I <u>learned</u> in school that poison ivy has three leaves.

Poison ivy

3 Make an Inference

Combine what you observe with what you know. Then tell what you think happened.

The plant I saw is probably poison ivy.

4 Think It Through

After you make an inference, you should think about it. Did you consider all the facts? Does it make sense? Are there any other explanations that might make more sense?

TIP An inference is not always correct. After you make an inference, you can test it to see if you are correct.

EXAMPLE OF Inferring
Read what one student inferred.

Observe → A green vine with five leaves is growing along the fence in my backyard.

Use what you know → It looks like poison ivy I saw when I was on a hike with my scout troop. My scout leader told us to remember the saying "leaves of three, let them be" so that we wouldn't touch poison ivy.

I don't think that the plant is poison ivy because it has five leaves. Poison ivy has only three leaves. ← **Infer**

Think it through → I looked for the plant in a book I have about plants. I was right. The plant is not poison ivy. It is Virginia creeper, a plant that many people confuse with poison ivy. Virginia creeper won't give me an itchy rash.

USE THIS SKILL
Infer

Read the notes that one student wrote. Then answer the questions.

Hike through Miller's Forest

On a hike, I stopped to look at a tree that was covered with a green vine. While I was standing there, I saw a wood rat eating leaves from the vine. It ran away really fast when I moved. After the rat ran away, I decided to find out more about the vine that was growing on the tree. I looked closer and I could see that the vine had three leaves and white, waxy looking berries. I was sure that the vine was poison ivy. I wondered how a rat could eat poison ivy.

I remembered that when I touched poison ivy before, it made me itch and I got a rash. It seemed like a rat would itch too. Then I remembered that my teacher said that the oil from poison ivy does not hurt most animals. She said that many kinds of birds and deer eat poison ivy leaves and berries. I decided that wood rats must be able to eat poison ivy too. The oil must not affect them.

1. What did the student observe?
2. What did the student wonder?
3. What did the student know about poison ivy?
4. How did that information help the student understand the situation?
5. What did the student infer?

TEST TIP On a test you may be asked to read a passage and make an inference. Use the information from the passage and what you already know to make an inference.

Skill 19
HOW TO
Make a Decision

Choosing a Science Fair Project

It's that time of year again—time for the science fair. What will you do for your science fair project? There are so many choices, it can be hard to decide which one is right for you.

You make decisions every day. A **decision** is a choice you make. Some decisions, such as what to have for breakfast are easily made. Others, such as how to spend your allowance or which science fair project to do, are more complicated and more difficult. Making good decisions is important to your health, happiness, and well-being.

A good decision is one you can live with and learn from. Use the steps on the next page to help you make decisions.

STEPS IN Making a Decision

1 Set Goals

Think about what you want to accomplish. Identify what is important to you. Write your goals.

My goals for the science fair:
- Learn more about health
- Do something different from everybody else
- Win a ribbon

2 Identify Choices

There are many ways you can go about reaching your goals. Before you make a decision, you need to list as many of these choices as you can. After you have listed all the choices you can think of, ask for ideas from your family members, teachers, and friends.

3 Consider Choices

Next to each choice you listed write advantages, or what is good about that choice, as well as disadvantages or drawbacks. You may ask yourself, Do I have enough time for this? Will the information or materials be hard to find? Will it be expensive? Am I really interested in this? What are the consequences of not doing this? Consider facts as well as your own feelings. You can make a chart to help you organize and consider your choices.

4 Make a Decision

Look at the chart you made. Think through the advantages and disadvantages of each choice. Then decide which choice is best for you.

EXAMPLE OF Making a Decision

Read the chart below. See how one student used the decision-making process to choose a science fair project.

Possible Science Fair Projects		
Projects	Advantages	Disadvantages
Survey how much time classmates spend on exercise and other activities *(Identify choices)*	I could make a graph for my display. It would be easy to survey my classmates in time for the science fair.	It seems like I wouldn't have enough information to fill a display. I wouldn't get to build anything.
Model of Food Guide Pyramid	It might help me remember number of servings better. I like building things.	The materials may be expensive or hard to find. A lot of students do this.
Display of healthful snacks	It would help me choose better snacks. It might help others too.	I'm not really interested in this. This seems too easy. *(Feeling)*
Find out my heart rate during different activities *(Decision)*	I would learn which activities raise my heart rate the most. I could make a graph or a table. I could include photographs of myself doing the different activities.	I will have to ask someone to take my picture while I do the different activities. *(Fact)*

USE THIS SKILL
Make a Decision

Read the ideas for science fair projects below. Make a chart to help you decide which one you would most like to do.

Science Fair Ideas

Make a model of a heart
Design an improved piece of safety equipment
Show how to properly care for teeth
Investigate how well people can detect different smells
Show why illegal drugs are harmful
Investigate how much starch is in certain foods

TEST TIP You may be asked to answer multiple-choice questions on a test. Read all the choices. Decide which ones are definitely wrong first. Then decide which of the other answer choices is best.

Skill 20
HOW TO
Work in a Group

Making a Terrarium

A **terrarium** is a clear container in which small plants or land animals can live. Making one can be a big job. Doing it as a group project makes it easier. When you **work in a group**, you have to help each other reach a goal. You have to make choices and decisions together.

Making a terrarium can be useful for your whole class. A terrarium is a good way to study small plants or animals. It is its own little ecosystem. If properly made and cared for, it will provide a good home for plants or animals. Working together as a group to make a terrarium will require you to make a plan and then carry it out. Follow the steps on the next page to learn how to work in a group.

STEPS IN Working in a Group

1 Set a Goal

Your group should begin by talking about your project. Be sure that all group members understand both the assignment and the goal. During your discussion, everyone should be able to share his or her ideas. Listening carefully is important. Then try to reach a decision with which all group members agree. When you reach a group decision about your goal, write it down.

2 Divide and Assign Tasks

Now your group can decide what needs to be done to achieve the goal. Each group member must choose a task or job to do. Divide the work as evenly as possible.

TIP Here's how to be a good listener. Look at the person speaking. Think about what the person is saying. Don't interrupt.

3 Make a Schedule

Group members should agree when they will complete each task. Write down a schedule for when each task will be finished. Keep to the schedule.

4 Share Responsibilities

Sometimes a task turns out to be too much for one person. Sometimes part of one task turns out to be the same as part of another task. If either of these things happens, revise your plan so that all group members share equally in the responsibilities.

EXAMPLE OF Working in a Group

Read this group plan for making a desert terrarium.

	Group Plan
Goal →	**A.** Our project is to make a desert terrarium for our classroom. Our group will gather the materials and build the terrarium.
Tasks →	**B. Things we need to do:**
	• Get an old aquarium, pebbles, sandy soil, plants (cactus, aloe, and sedum), interesting-looking small stones, and rocks.
	• Put a layer of pebbles and then a layer of sandy soil in the aquarium.
	• Plant the plants, and water them just a little.
Jobs →	• Add the stones and rocks.
	• Clean up the mess.
	C. Jobs for each group member:
	name: <u>Kim</u> Job: <u>Get pebbles and soil. Layer them in aquarium.</u>
	name: <u>Ramon</u> Job: <u>Get plants. Plant them in aquarium and water them.</u>
	name: <u>Beverlee</u> Job: <u>Get rocks and stones. Arrange them in aquarium.</u>
Schedule →	names: <u>Kim, Ramon, Beverlee</u> Job: <u>Clean up your part of the mess.</u>
	D. Schedule:
	Job: Get pebbles and soil. Put in aquarium.
	Due Date: October 7

USE THIS SKILL

Work in a Group

Work with a group of classmates to make a woodland terrarium. You will need a clear plastic container. You will also need pebbles, small pieces of charcoal, soil, plants, water, and a lid for the terrarium. You can use the plan below to help you write a plan for your group.

Group Plan

A. Our project is _____

B. Things we need to do: _____

C. Jobs for each group member: _____
   Name: _____ Job: _____

D. Schedule: _____
   Job: _____ Date Due: _____

E. Adjustments to plan: _____

TEST TIP When you take tests, use the time you have in the best way. Go through the test once answering all the questions you know right away. Then go back to the ones that are more difficult.

Skill 21
HOW TO
Make a Learning Log

Life at the Vents

There is probably no alien world you can imagine that would look stranger than the deepest parts of the ocean.

Scientists have recently begun to explore the bottom layer of the ocean. One of the biggest surprises in this exploration was the discovery of hydrothermal vents. **Hydrothermal vents** are openings on the ocean floor. Hot, mineral-rich water spews out of these openings. This water contains chemicals that support a variety of organisms. Hydrothermal vents form when seawater seeps into openings in the ocean floor. This water is heated by magma, or hot molten rock, beneath Earth's crust. As the water is heated, pressure forces the water through openings in the ocean floor.

Giant tube worms

When you are reading about topics such as hydrothermal vents, it can be useful to write your thoughts about what you are reading. You can do this by making a learning log. A **learning log** is a journal in which you write about what you are studying. You can write questions, ideas that interest you, drawings and definitions of words.

STEPS IN Making a Learning Log

1 Choose Your Subjects

Think about your school subjects. Which ones do you find really interesting? Which ones do you find difficult? You could do a learning log for any or all of them. Choose one or more of your subjects for your learning log.

2 Make Your Log

You can use a notebook that has dividers. You can just staple some sheets of paper together to make your learning log. It does not matter what it looks like. What matters is that you have a place to write about each subject you choose. Write the name of each subject on the first page of each section of your learning log.

3 Find Time to Write

It is a good idea to choose a time each day to write in your learning log. Getting into a routine will make it easier to do. Try to think of it as time for yourself. This is a time to record your thoughts and opinions about what you are learning.

4 Relax When You Write

No one will read your log but you. The learning log is a chance for you to explore what interests you, puzzles you, and causes you to ask questions.

> **TIP** It is a good idea to write the date of each entry in your learning log. Then you will have a clearer picture of how your thoughts change over time.

EXAMPLE OF Making a Learning Log

Read the passage below. Then read the learning log entry. Notice the different reactions the student had to what she read.

Living by a Vent

There probably is not a more difficult place to live on Earth than a hydrothermal vent. To begin with, there is no light in the deep ocean. It is completely black. Then, there is the pressure—more than 3,350 pounds per square inch in some places. On top of that, there are both extremely cold and extremely hot temperatures to deal with. The mixture of water and chemicals coming out of one of these vents can be hot enough to melt lead. The surrounding ocean water stays at about 35 degrees Fahrenheit. The organisms that live at a vent exist in total darkness, under intense pressure, and endure extreme temperatures. It seems an impossible place to survive, but they do.

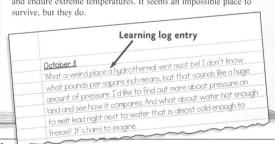

Learning log entry

October 8
What a weird place a hydrothermal vent must be! I don't know what pounds per square inch means, but that sounds like a huge amount of pressure. I'd like to find out more about pressure on land and see how it compares. And what about water hot enough to melt lead right next to water that is almost cold enough to freeze? It's hard to imagine.

USE THIS SKILL
Make a Learning Log
Read the passage below. Then write a learning log entry.

Vent Life

The organisms that live around hydrothermal vents are like nothing else on Earth. There are shrimp with no eyes, huge white crabs, clams, giant tube worms that can be more than 10 feet long, snails with no shells, fish that look like snakes, and white bacteria that form mats on the ocean floor several inches thick. So far, more than 300 species have been identified living around the vents. Scientists did not know that more than 95 percent of these species existed until recently. Who knows what else is down there?

> **TEST TIP** On some tests you may be asked to respond to a passage you have read. Think about the question or directions carefully. Keep them in mind when you read the passage. Your response should answer the question or follow the directions.

Skill 22
HOW TO
Write a Paragraph

National Parks in Trouble

Yosemite National Park was created more than 100 years ago. Over the years, presidents set aside the nation's finest land so that visitors could enjoy the beautiful scenery.

Yosemite National Park

Today many of the national parks, while still beautiful, are in trouble. The parks are often overcrowded because so many people visit them. Cars cause pollution in the very places that were set aside for quiet and clean air. The parks system is also running out of money. When short of money, the parks can't make repairs and problems become worse. People have different ideas about how to save the parks. Some businesses would like to fix up the parks and build more motels and restaurants. Some people think the parks should charge a fee to visit the parks. Others think the number of visitors allowed in the parks should be limited.

If you wanted to persuade people to save the national parks, you could write a paragraph explaining your opinion. A **paragraph** is a group of sentences about a single idea.

STEPS IN Writing a Paragraph

1 Write a Topic Sentence

The **topic sentence** of a paragraph is the sentence that tells the main idea. The topic sentence is often the first sentence of a paragraph. When writing a paragraph to persuade, state your opinion on the subject in the topic sentence. Write the topic sentence without using the pronoun *I*.

Helicopter rides over the Grand Canyon should be stopped.

2 Add Facts

To persuade your readers to accept an opinion, you must give them the facts. Follow your topic sentence with several sentences containing facts that support your opinion.

So many helicopters fly over the Grand Canyon each day that visitors on the ground hear noise all day long.

3 Write a Conclusion

Save your best reasons for your opinion for the last sentence of your paragraph. You can also end your paragraph with a sentence that sums up the reasons for your opinion.

Banning helicopters will reduce noise pollution and allow tourists to enjoy a quiet day in the wilderness.

Grand Canyon

EXAMPLE OF Writing a Paragraph

As you read the following paragraph, notice how the writer's opinion is supported by facts.

Problems in Yosemite National Park

Topic sentence → To save the environment, cars should be banned from Yosemite National Park. **Supporting sentences →** Each year, more than three million people visit this spectacular park in California. They bring thousands of cars into the park each day. The cars fill the few roads in the park, causing traffic jams. Air pollution from these cars creates smog that harms the tourists as well as plants and animals. The many automobiles also cause noise pollution, so tourists can't hear the birds or the waterfalls. **Conclusion sentence →** Banning cars and bringing tourists into the park in buses is the best solution to the problems of traffic jams and air pollution in Yosemite National Park.

USE THIS SKILL
Write a Paragraph

Research a problem at one of the national parks below. Then write a persuasive paragraph. Describe the problem and tell how you think the problem should be solved.

- Joshua Tree National Monument in California
- Great Smoky Mountains National Park in Tennessee
- Shenandoah National Park in Virginia
- Cape Cod National Seashore in Massachusetts
- Petroglyph National Monument in New Mexico
- Hawaii Volcanoes National Park in Hawaii
- Indiana Dunes National Lakeshore in Indiana
- Acadia National Park in Maine

TEST TIP If you are asked to write a persuasive paragraph for a test, choose a topic you understand. Use facts to support your opinion. Write clearly so that the reader will understand your point of view.

Skill 23
HOW TO
Write an Outline

Natural Resources

Imagine what it would be like to live without water, wood, and soil. Think about how living without electricity or gasoline would change your life. Life would be very different without natural resources like these.

A **natural resource** is any material that comes from Earth, such as natural gas, wood, and oil. Some natural resources are called **renewable resources** because they cannot be used up. Power that comes from wind, water, and the sun are examples of renewable resources.

Early people used sails on ships to use the power of the wind. American pioneers built windmills to pump water and

Wind farm

grind grain. Today's windmills are used to generate electricity at wind farms. Humans have also used the power of falling water. Waterwheels were used for centuries to drive machines, such as mills or grindstones. Today the term **hydroelectric power** is used to describe the production of energy from flowing water at dams. When water from a dam is released, its energy is used to turn turbines that convert the energy into electricity.

Energy from the sun, or solar energy, can also be collected and used to heat homes and generate electricity. One way to collect solar energy is to use large mirrors that reflect sunlight. This sunlight heats a tank of water, causing it to boil. The steam from the boiling water can be converted into electricity.

Other natural resources are called nonrenewable because their supply is limited. **Nonrenewable resources** are natural resources that cannot be replaced. Fossil fuels such as coal, oil, and natural gas are nonrenewable resources.

Suppose you want to write about natural resources. To organize your facts before you begin to write, you can make an outline. An **outline** is a written plan to organize information into main ideas and details. Using an outline will help you as you write. Use the steps on the next page to help you write an outline.

House with solar panels

STEPS IN Writing an Outline

1 Write the Topic

Write the topic of your outline at the top of the page. This is the title of your outline.

2 Organize Your Notes

Before you begin your outline, read about your topic and take notes. Then look over your notes to find the main ideas. **Main ideas** are the most important facts about a topic. Circle or highlight the main ideas in your notes.

Oil rig

3 Write the Main Ideas

In your outline, write the main ideas in a word or short phrase. You do not need to write in complete sentences. Use Roman numerals to number each of your main ideas. Leave several lines between the main ideas.

   I. Renewable Resources
   II. Nonrenewable Resources

4 Add Details

On the lines below each main idea write details about that main idea. Indent each line and use capital letters to begin each detail that tells about the main idea.

Remember that no numeral or letter can stand alone in an outline. Each must be paired with at least one other numeral or letter. If you have a I, you must also have a II. If you have an A, you must also have a B. You can use as many numerals or letters as you need to complete the ideas.

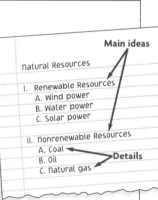

TIP Roman numerals are a different way of numbering that was used by the Roman Empire more than 2,000 years ago. These Roman numerals are for the numbers 1 through 5:

I = 1   IV = 4
II = 2   V = 5
III = 3

EXAMPLE OF Writing an Outline

As you read the outline below look for the title, main ideas, and details. Notice that words or phrases, not complete sentences, are used in this outline.

```
Main ideas ──→  ──Title
               Fossil Fuels
                  I. Coal
                     A. Solid material formed from dead plants
                     B. Mined, or removed from the ground
                     C. Used to fuel electric power plants today ──Details
                 II. Oil
                     A. Thick, black liquid
                     B. Also called petroleum
                     C. Usually located deep underground
                III. Natural Gas
                     A. A mixture of gases
                     B. Often found above an oil deposit
                     C. Transported in pipelines
```

USE THIS SKILL
Write an Outline

The note cards below discuss the advantages and disadvantages of using coal. Read the note cards. Then make an outline of the information.

Advantages of using coal
- Coal creates a lot of energy when burned.
- It can be transported easily to places where it is needed.
- There is more coal in the United States than any other fossil fuel.
- Mining coal provides jobs for many people.

Disadvantages of using coal
- Burning coal causes air pollution.
- Mining coal can cause land to erode.
- Water in the mines can run into other water sources, polluting them.
- Some coal is mixed with other materials, making it hard to mine.
- Coal mining can be a dangerous job.

TEST TIP You may be asked to write an essay on a test. Before you begin to write, organize your ideas by creating an outline on scratch paper. Then follow your outline as you write your essay.

Skill 24
HOW TO Write a Summary

Are There Microbes in Your Future?

If you like science, you might consider becoming a **microbiologist.** That's a person who studies **microbes,** tiny organisms that can be seen only with a microscope. Think about it. You'd be like an explorer in a world most people never see. You might even discover new life forms that no one knew existed. You might find yourself looking for clues to defeat disease-causing germs. It could be quite an adventure.

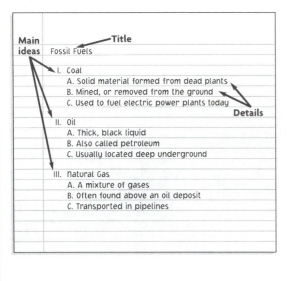

Listeria bacteria

The paragraph you just read is a summary of some of the things microbiologists do, and it doesn't give many details. A **summary** is a collection of main ideas about a topic. Writing a summary can help you remember important ideas. It can help you review and remember a book, an article, a story, or a lesson. The steps on the next two pages will help you write a summary.

STEPS IN Writing a Summary

1 Read Carefully

Read the passage that you would like to summarize. Look for main ideas. They tell you what the passage is about. As you read, look for answers to questions such as Who, What, When, Where, Why, and How. Now read the passage carefully again. Take notes if you wish.

2 Plan Your Summary

First, identify topic sentences. A topic sentence contains the main idea of the paragraph. The other sentences in the paragraph give details, examples, and reasons that support the main idea.

The topic sentence in the following paragraph, which is highlighted in blue, contains the main idea of the paragraph. The rest of the sentences give more information about the main idea.

What Do Microbiologists Do?

Microbiologists spend some of their time in a lab looking at slides under a microscope, but that is just part of what they do. Some travel to far-off jungles to look for new kinds of microbes. Others find themselves underwater learning about sea microbes. Still others go to deserts or arctic regions to study microbes that can live in extreme temperatures. Because microbes are everywhere in the world, microbiologists can work just about anywhere.

If you identify and list all the topic sentences in a reading, you will have some of the main ideas. Then you can choose the main ideas that you want to include in your summary.

3 Write a Draft

Organize the main ideas you have selected in the order that you want them to appear in your summary. Use only important information. Begin writing your summary, being certain to include the most important idea from the reading in your first sentence. Use your own words. Write complete sentences.

4 Revise and Edit Your Draft

Read your draft. Did you include the important ideas? If not, add them. Did you include any details, examples, or reasons? If you did include them, cross them out. Details, examples, and reasons should not be part of a summary. To **revise** is to make these kinds of changes. After you have made them, **edit** your work by correcting any mistakes in spelling, punctuation, and use of capital letters.

5 Publish Your Summary

Write a final draft, including all corrections. If you are writing by hand, neatly copy your summary onto a clean sheet of paper. If you are using a computer, you can just make changes to your draft document before printing and saving your revision.

TIP Look for boldface headings in a reading. These may tell you what the main ideas are. You can also check the table of contents. It may help you find the main ideas in a book.

EXAMPLE OF Writing a Summary

Read this passage about careers in microbiology. Then read the example summary on the next page.

Topic sentence

Careers in Microbiology

If you decide to become a microbiologist, you will need to choose an area in which to work. There are many different kinds of microbes. It would be impossible to study them all so you will have to select one area. You may even be able to match some of your other interests with the area of microbiology you choose. ← Topic sentence

Medical microbiologists study how microbes cause diseases in humans and animals. They look for cures. They also look for ways to prevent diseases from occurring. Their work has led to the discovery of vaccines and other medicines that can protect us from many diseases. ← Topic sentence

Marine microbiologists deal with microbes found in the ocean. This is one of the newer areas of microbiology. We know far less about microbes in the ocean than we do about microbes on land. People doing this work are on the frontier of microbiology. ← Topic sentence

Agricultural microbiologists study how microbes affect the growth and storage of farm products. They are interested in plant diseases caused by microbes. They are also interested in the effect microbes have on soil, and they want to know how and why food spoils. These microbiologists keep looking for ways to help farmers increase their crops and keep the food supply safe.

EXAMPLE OF Writing a Summary

Read the example summary below. Notice that it contains the main ideas of the passage on page 117.

Most important idea

Microbiologists work in many different areas. Medical microbiologists study how microbes cause diseases in humans and animals. Marine microbiologists study microbes that live in the ocean. Agricultural microbiologists study how microbes affect farm products.

USE THIS SKILL

Write a Summary

Write a summary of the following passage.

Preparing to Become a Microbiologist

There are several steps to becoming a microbiologist, and you can get started right away. Look for information and resources that are available in your school and community. Ask your science teacher to help you do experiments with microbes. Ask a librarian to help you find books on life sciences and microbiology. Get involved in science fairs. Visit a science museum.

When you get to high school, choose subjects that will help you when you get to college. Take as many biology, chemistry, computer sciences, and mathematics courses as you can. Do not forget to keep working on your reading skills. You will need to be a good reader to understand all the materials in your college textbooks.

At college, decide exactly what you want to do and work toward a degree that will allow you to reach your goal. There are degrees that take two years, four years, five years, and eight years to complete. Each of these degrees will prepare you for specific jobs in the field of microbiology.

TEST TIP Some tests may ask you to summarize something you have read. Write your summary in your own words. Try to be as brief as possible without leaving out any important ideas.

Skill 25
HOW TO
Write a Description

Yellowstone's Hot Springs

Yellowstone National Park covers more than 3,000 square miles of land where the states of Montana, Idaho, and Wyoming meet. If you visit Yellowstone National Park, you can see the world's most famous hot springs.

A spring is any flow of water from the Earth. Water in hot springs is heated by geothermal energy. *Geo* means "Earth." *Thermal* means "warm." **Geothermal energy** is thermal energy that comes from Earth. Temperatures deep in Earth's surface are hot enough to melt rock. The temperatures can also heat water.

Hot springs form when cracks in hot rocks underground lead to Earth's surface. When water fills these cracks, the water boils, creating steam. Steam bubbles up from the cracks in the rock, forming a pool of hot water. Hot springs vary in temperature from 116 °F to 212 °F, or boiling.

Silex Spring

Geysers are a kind of hot spring known for violent eruptions. When pressure from steam builds up in a crack in hot rock, the hot water and steam occasionally are thrown up into the air. Some geysers erupt every minute, while others may be inactive for months or even years.

Mud pots are another type of hot spring. A mud pot is formed when the hot water from a spring mixes with clay or other minerals. The hot water may occasionally cause mud to be flung into the air. Depending on the kind of minerals, mud pots can be colorful. For this reason, they are sometimes called paint pots.

Fumaroles are hot springs that are dry but release steam. Water vapor and other gases burst from holes in the ground. Fumaroles are sometimes called "dry geysers" because they explode with such force that the ground trembles and roars.

You can learn a lot about a topic such as hot springs from a written description. A **description** gives details about a person, place, object, or action. Good descriptions help readers create pictures in their minds. Follow the steps on the next page to learn how to write descriptions.

STEPS IN Writing a Description

1 Plan Your Paragraph

Before you begin writing, plan your paragraph.

Choose a topic.
A good topic can be described not only by how it looks but also by how it feels, sounds, tastes, and smells. Make sure that you have enough information to write a paragraph.

List describing words.
Brainstorm a list of words and phrases you can use to describe your topic. Write them on a piece of paper. Descriptive language will bring your writing to life. Focus on choosing:

Nouns—Choose specific words to name a person, place, object, or action:

The <u>eruption</u> shook the ground.

TIP To find the best describing word, use a thesaurus. A thesaurus is a book that contains lists of synonyms. For example, look up the word **beautiful**. The listing will give you many choices, such as **elegant, stunning, sublime,** and **superb.**

Verbs—Choose strong words to show an action:

The fumarole <u>hissed</u> and <u>groaned</u>.

Adjectives—Choose colorful words to describe nouns:

<u>Thick, orange</u> mud swirled in the pool.

Adverbs—Choose accurate words to describe verbs:

Old Faithful erupts <u>violently</u> every 65 minutes.

2 Write a Draft

Start with a topic sentence that tells your readers what the paragraph is about. Then add details to provide more information about your topic. Be sure to include the describing words from your list. Skip lines when writing the draft, so you'll have space to make changes later.

3 Revise Your Draft

Now read your paragraph to make sure that it makes sense. Ask yourself if your writing is easy to understand. Consider replacing some words with more descriptive words or adding more details. You might also ask a partner to read it and make comments. Then make any changes that improve your paragraph.

4 Edit and Publish

Look closely at the revised draft of your paragraph. Check for mistakes in grammar, spelling, and punctuation. Once you have made all the necessary changes, neatly write or type your paragraph on a clean sheet of paper.

Old Faithful geyser

EXAMPLE OF Writing a Description

As you read the description below look for descriptive words.

Fountain Paint Pot

Fountain Paint Pot is located along a trail in the Lower Geyser Basin of Yellowstone National Park. <u>Colorful, hot</u> mud <u>bubbles</u> in Fountain Paint Pot all day long. Many years ago, steam released underwater created an acid that turned the solid rock into clay. Today the steam <u>bursts</u> through the <u>soft</u> clay, causing the bubbling action of the mud. Pressure from the steam occasionally <u>throws gobs</u> of mud up to 20 feet into the air. When it rains, the paint pot becomes <u>soupy</u>. As the pool dries, the mud becomes <u>thick</u> again. Fountain Paint Pot is best viewed in winter when <u>melting</u> snow produces the perfect conditions for seeing the famous, <u>bubbling mud</u>.

← Descriptive words

Fountain Paint Pot

USE THIS SKILL
Write a Description

Choose one of the following geothermal wonders from Yellowstone National Park. Research the hot spring you choose and write a paragraph to describe it.

Hot Springs

- Great Fountain geyser
- Old Faithful geyser
- Grand Prismatic Spring
- Red Spouter
- Celestine Pool
- Excelsior geyser
- Mammoth Hot Springs
- Mud Volcano

TEST TIP You may be asked to write a description on a test. Use colorful words to help the reader understand what you are describing.

Skill 26
HOW TO
Write a Comparison/Contrast

Improving Technology Improves Health

You have changed over the years. You are taller than you used to be. Your feet are bigger. You can read and write now. However, some things about you are still the same. You might live in the same place or go to the same school you went to last year.

You are not the only thing that changes over time. Inventions change too. Often, with new technology, new inventions are made or devices are improved. This is certainly the case with artificial limbs, or **prostheses**.

People who are born without arms, legs, hands, or feet or lose them through accidents or disease can lead healthy, active lives with the use of modern prostheses.

Artificial limbs have been used for thousands of years. Do you suppose today's prostheses are more similar or more different from the earlier ones? You might be surprised. In some ways they have changed a great deal. In other ways they are much the same as they used to be.

A good way to more fully understand two or more topics is to compare and contrast them. To **compare** means to tell how two things are the same. To **contrast** means to tell how two things are different.

When you write a comparison/contrast paragraph, you must choose your topics carefully. The two topics you choose must be related somehow. For example, you could easily compare old prosthetic devices to new ones because they are alike in some ways. However, you probably would not compare a jet to an ocean. These two topics are too different to be compared. You can follow the steps on the next page to write a comparison/contrast.

This basketball player wears a prosthesis.

STEPS IN Writing a Comparison/Contrast

1 Choose Topics

Think about people, places, things, or events you would like to compare and contrast. The two topics should be the same in some ways and different in others. Try to choose topics that you find interesting.

2 Gather Information

Find out more about your topics. You can look for information in encyclopedias, newspapers, magazines, and on the Internet. Take notes in your own words to remind you of what you have read.

3 Make a Chart

Read over your notes and decide what is the same and what is different about your topics. You can sort the information in a T-chart to help you organize your thoughts before you write.

Prostheses, Old and New

Same	Different
Replace missing limbs	Old—made of leather, wood, iron
	New—made of metals and plastic
	Old—heavy
	New—lightweight
	Old—made by craftspeople
	New—made by biomedical engineers

4 Use Signal Words

Signal words can help your reader know which traits are the same and which are different. Signal words such as *both, also, similar, same, as,* and *like* can tell how topics are similar. Signal words such as *unlike, but, more, less, better, worse,* and *different* can tell how topics are different.

Both old and new prostheses were developed to help people.

Early prosthetic legs were heavy, but today they are made of lightweight materials.

TIP Write a strong topic sentence for your paragraph. It should tell the reader the topics you are comparing and contrasting in your paragraph. All the other sentences in the paragraph should tell more about the topic sentence.

5 Use Adjectives

You can choose adjectives carefully to show how your topics are different. Words that end in *–er* such as *thicker* or *smarter* compare two subjects. Words that end in *–est* such as *smallest* and *loudest* compare three or more subjects. Adjectives used to contrast sometimes use the word *more*.

Artificial legs used to be heavier than they are now.

The greatest changes in prostheses have occurred since World War II.

Biomedical engineers are more knowledgeable about how the body works than people who made prostheses many years ago.

EXAMPLE OF Writing a Comparison/Contrast

Read the following paragraph. Notice how old and new prostheses are the same and how they are different.

Artificial Legs, Past and Present

Topic sentence → Prosthetic limbs have changed a lot in 2,000 years, but some things about them have not changed. **Compares →** Like artificial limbs of the past, today's prostheses replace natural limbs that have been lost through accidents or disease. In the past, craftspeople such as clockmakers or locksmiths often made prosthetic legs because they had the skills to work with wood, leather, and metal. Today they are made by biomedical engineers who know a great deal about how the body moves and works as well as new and changing technology. **← Contrasts** Long ago, prosthetic legs were made to look like natural legs, but they were heavy and did not move well. Today, they are made to actually perform more like a human leg. This way they can better fit the needs of the wearer. Lighter metals and better technology make it possible for wearers to run races, play sports, and enjoy healthy, active lifestyles.

USE THIS SKILL

Write a Comparison/Contrast

Look at the pictures below. Use the pictures to write one paragraph that compares and contrasts the runners.

TEST TIP You may be asked to write a comparison/contrast on a test. Make sure you tell what is the same as well as what is different about the two subjects.

Skill 27
HOW TO
Write about a Process

Glass: A "Super Cool" Matter

Is glass a solid or a liquid? If you said liquid you are right! Even though glass feels hard, it is not a solid.

Glass is a supercooled liquid. **Supercooled liquids** look solid but act like liquids or solids depending on their temperatures. When very hot, they resemble liquids. When they cool, they are more like solids. Think about how butter appears after it is heated. Then think about how butter appears and feels after being chilled in a refrigerator. Glass is much the same way. When glass is heated it gradually softens. The hotter it gets, the more easily glass flows. As glass cools, it flows more slowly. At room temperature, glass flows so slowly that it appears to be solid. This characteristic allows artists to shape melted glass yet have a finished product that seems solid.

To understand how artists work with glass, you can write about the process of glassblowing. To **write about a process** means to write a step-by-step explanation that tells how something is done. Use the steps on the next page to write about a process.

STEPS IN Writing about a Process

1 Gather Information

Gather information about your topic from a variety of sources. Take notes on what you read.

2 Get Organized

Create a numbered list or flowchart of the steps in the process. This will allow you to make sure that no steps have been left out.

3 Write a Draft

Begin with a topic sentence that tells the subject of your paragraph. Then explain the steps. Include **sequence words** such as *first, next, then, after, before,* and *finally* to help the reader follow the steps. Explain the meanings of any words the reader may not know.

4 Revise and Edit

After you write your draft, read it carefully. Check that your ideas are clear and the steps are written in the correct order. Look for mistakes in spelling, grammar, and punctuation. Make any necessary changes. Then make a final, neat copy of your draft.

How Artists Blow Glass
1. The artist heats the end of a blowpipe until it is hot.
2. The artist dips the end of the blowpipe into melted glass.
3. The artist gathers glass into a blob on the end of the blowpipe.
4. The artist blows into the end of the blowpipe to make a bubble in the glass.
5. The artist puts the bubble back into the furnace to gather up more glass.
6. Steps 4 and 5 are repeated several times.
7. The artist rotates the blowpipe so that the glass does not flow off the pipe.

EXAMPLE OF Writing about a Process

Read the following explanation of glassblowing. Notice how the writer uses sequence words.

Topic sentence →

How Artists Blow Glass

It takes patience and skill to blow glass. <u>First</u> the artist heats the end of a pipe, called a blowpipe, until it is very hot. <u>Then</u> the artist dips the hot end of the blowpipe into melted glass that is kept inside a furnace. The artist gathers glass into a blob on the end of the blowpipe. <u>Next</u> the artist blows air through the pipe to form a thick bubble in the glass. <u>Then</u> the artist puts the bubble back into the furnace to gather up more glass. The artist will usually blow into the pipe and gather more glass several times before beginning the next step. The artist also rotates the blowpipe so that the glass does not flow off the pipe. <u>Next</u> the artist shapes the hot glass using sticks, pliers, or other tools. While the glass is being shaped, the glass must often be reheated inside a very hot furnace called a glory hole. This keeps the glass in a liquid state as it is shaped. <u>Then</u> the artist removes the glass from the pipe. Next the glass is put onto an iron rod called a punty. The punty allows the artist to open the glass to make the mouth of a bowl or vase. <u>Finally</u> when the piece is finished, the artist carefully breaks it off the punty. The piece is put in an oven where it slowly cools to room temperature.

Sequence words

USE THIS SKILL
Write about a Process

Cooking is a process that involves heating and cooling. Choose one of the topics below and write about the process.

- Making fudge
- Baking bread
- Making pudding
- Making a gelatin dessert
- Making peanut brittle
- Making popcorn

TEST TIP: A test may have questions about a reading passage that includes the steps in a process. Watch for sequence words to help you know the correct order of the steps.

Skill 28
HOW TO Use the Library

Volcanoes

The students in Mr. Blackmore's class were studying volcanoes. They read about how volcanoes form and what happens when they erupt.

A **volcano** is an opening in Earth's crust where molten material called magma comes to the surface. Magma is a mixture of melted rock, water, and gases. The gases in magma are under pressure. As magma reaches the surface, the gases begin to form bubbles. When a volcano erupts, the gases in the magma rush out carrying the magma with them. Magma that reaches the surface is called **lava.** Lava can flow through cracks in the side of a volcano or shoot out the top of a volcano. The hot lava, gases, ash, and rock from a volcano can destroy whatever is nearby.

The students had many questions about volcanoes, so they went to the library to do some research. A **library** is a collection of books and other materials that is organized to make finding information easy.

How many kinds of volcanoes are there?
What does the inside of a volcano look like?
Where are most volcanoes found?
How often do volcanoes erupt?

STEPS IN Using the Library

1 Search for Information

To help you search, your library will provide either a card catalog or a computer catalog. A **card catalog** is a collection of small file drawers full of cards containing information about books and other materials in the library. Each source is listed three ways: by title, author, and subject. The cards are filed in alphabetical order. If you wanted to find a book on volcanoes, you would search in the subject drawer under the Vs, looking for the word *volcano*.

A **computer catalog** provides the same kind of information. Each computer catalog is a bit different. You will probably be asked whether you want to find a source by its title, author, or subject. To find sources on volcanoes, you will probably click on the word *SUBJECT*, then type in the word *volcano*. This list shows the sources a library has on volcanoes. To learn where a source is located, click on the title.

SUBJECT: Volcanoes	Source	Year
Atlas of Volcanic Landforms on Mars/Carroll Ann Hodges	Book	1994
Fire on the Mountain: The Nature of Volcanoes/Carl Johnson; photographs by Dorian Weisel	Book	1994
Volcano!/Ellen J. Prager	Juvenile book	2001
Volcanoes/Robert Decker and Barbara Decker	Book and CD-ROM	1998

2 Locate the Source

Nonfiction books are filed on library shelves according to **call numbers** written on the book's spine. The numbers are usually based on the Dewey Decimal System. A library may add abbreviations to provide further information about where a source is located. A book with a *J* before the call number, for example, can be found in the Juvenile section.

Common abbreviations are:

J juvenile
O oversize
REF reference
VID video

The screen above shows the listing for a book about volcanoes. Call numbers tell you where to look in the library to find the book.

Author: Prager, Ellen J.
Title: Volcano!
Call Number: J 521.3P
Publisher: Washington, D.C.: National Geographic Society, 2001
Description: This book gives basic information on volcanoes and describes the different kinds of volcanoes.
Subjects: volcanoes – juvenile literature

The Ten Classes of the Dewey Decimal System

000 General Topics
100 Philosophy
200 Religion
300 The Social Sciences
400 Language
500 Pure Science
600 Technology (Applied Science)
700 The Arts, Recreation
800 Literature
900 Geography and History

3 Use the Source

After you find a book, use the table of contents or the index to help you find the information you need. The **table of contents** is found in the front of a book. It lists the chapters and sections, along with their beginning page numbers. An **index** is found in the back of the book. It lists subjects found in the book and the page number on which that information is found.

TIP Call numbers may contain decimals. The call number 521.18 is found on the shelf ahead of 521.3 because the 3 is actually 30 (without the 0 in the hundredths place).

Juvenile Section

EXAMPLE OF Using the Library

Ananda wanted to know what volcanic rocks look like. Read what Ananda did to find an answer to her question.

Ananda looked for a book in the card catalog at the library. First she looked for a book under the subject *volcanoes*. Then Ananda looked under the subject *rocks* and found this title:

Ananda used the book's index to find information about volcanic rocks. She found photographs of volcanic rock.

Title — *Volcanic Rocks* by Eduardo Carrillo — *Author*
O 714.5 — **Call number**
This book discusses rocks formed by volcanoes. Includes great photos!

Pumice
Obsidian
Basalt

Ananda wrote down the book's title, author, and call number. Then she went to the Oversize book section and found the book.

USE THIS SKILL
Use the Library

Choose one of the questions below or write your own question about volcanoes. Use the library to find an answer to your question. Write the call number and title of the source you use to find the answer.

Questions about Volcanoes

- What happens when a volcano erupts?
- What kind of volcano is Mount Saint Helens?
- What other planets have volcanoes?
- Why do some areas have more volcanoes than others?
- Which volcano is nearest to the place where you live?

TEST TIP
Some tests might ask you which part of a book you would use to answer a certain question. Remember that an appendix is a collection of extras, such as maps and charts. A glossary is a dictionary that defines words used in that book. A bibliography is a list of other sources you can read to find out more about your subject.

Skill 29
HOW TO
Write a Report

Pedal Power

Have you ever ridden a bicycle? Riding a bicycle can be a great way to exercise and get from place to place. You might be surprised to know that the bicycle was invented more than 200 years ago. But these first "bicycles" looked very different from the bicycles of today.

A **report** is a good way to find out more about a topic that you find interesting. Before you begin writing a report, choose a topic and jot down questions you would like to answer. You can use these steps to help you write a report.

1 Gather Information

After you choose your topic, you should collect information. Find as many sources of information as possible.

Ordinary

- When were bicycles invented?
- Who invented the earliest bicycles?
- What were old bicycles made of?
- What did old bicycles look like?
- How safe were old bicycles?
- How did bicycles change over time?

STEPS IN Writing a Report

Look for sources related to your topic.
You can start with an encyclopedia to get a general overview of your topic. Then find nonfiction books related to your topic. Nonfiction books will usually have more detailed information than an encyclopedia. You can also look for articles in newspapers and magazines as well as on the Internet. These sources tend to have more current information.

Keep notes.
Look for answers to your questions. Use the table of contents and index of each source you use to find important facts. Skim through a chapter or article to find keywords. When you find useful information, read it carefully and take notes. Be sure to write your notes in your own words.

Index cards are a great way to take notes. On each card write the name of the source you used. At the top of the card record a category that describes the notes on the index card. This will help you organize your notes.

Category
The Ordinary
- It became popular around 1874.
- It had a huge front wheel.
- It was a dangerous bike.
- Riders often flew over the front handlebars and suffered many injuries.

Notes
www.bikehistory.com
Source

STEPS IN Writing a Report

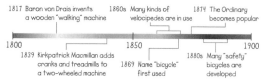

The History of Bicycles

- 1817 Baron von Drais invents a wooden "walking" machine
- 1839 Kirkpatrick Macmillan adds cranks and treadmills to a two-wheeled machine
- 1860s Many kinds of velocipedes are in use
- 1869 Name "bicycle" first used
- 1874 The Ordinary becomes popular
- 1880s Many "safety" bicycles are developed

2 Organize Your Information

Put your notes into categories.
Outlines, time lines, and idea webs are great ways to organize your notes.

3 Write the Report

Start with a draft.
Use your organized notes to write a draft. Your report should have a beginning, middle, and ending. Each paragraph should have a main idea and details that tell more about the main idea.

Beginning
This is the introduction to your topic. Try beginning with a question, a quote, or an interesting fact.

Middle
The middle should give more facts about your topic. You may wish to include pictures, charts, or diagrams.

Ending
The ending should "wrap up" your report.

Revise and edit your draft.
After you write a draft, you should read over your report.

Look for parts that are confusing or need more information. After you have made these changes, check your spelling, punctuation, and grammar. Then make a final, neat copy of your draft.

4 Include a Bibliography

List the sources you used.
At the end of your report you should list all the sources you used. This list of sources is called a **bibliography**. The sources are organized in alphabetical order by the authors' last names or the title if no author is listed. You can use the guide below to help you.

Book
Author's last name, author's first name. Title of Book. Name of publisher, copyright date.

Newspaper Article
Author's last name, author's first name. "Title of Article." Title of Newspaper. Volume number, issue number, page numbers of article.

Magazine Article
Author's last name, author's first name. "Title of Article." Title of Magazine. Date of magazine: page numbers of article.

Encyclopedia Article
Author (if given). "Title of Article." Title of Encyclopedia. Copyright date: page number of article.

Web Site
Author (if given). "Title of Article." Sponsor of Web site. Date of article. Web site address (URL).

EXAMPLE OF Writing a Report

Read the report below about the history of bicycles. Notice how the report is organized.

The History of Bicycles

Beginning
Aren't bikes great? After slipping on your helmet, you can hop on a bike and go. Bicycles as we know them have been more than 200 years in the making. Beginning with the idea that there must be an easier, more convenient way to get around, and after years of improvements, the bike as we know it was finally developed.

Middle
In 1817, Baron von Drais created a wooden machine that had two wheels of the same size. The rider had to straddle the machine and walk it. It must have been fairly safe because you could go only as fast as you could walk, but it was not very comfortable.

During the 1850s pedals were added to a two-wheeled machine. This machine was called a velocipede. The machine was also called a boneshaker because it was originally made of wood and the roads at the time were very bumpy. Later it had metal tires. Many kinds of velocipedes became popular during the 1860s.

A bicycle called the Ordinary became popular around 1874. It had a huge front wheel and was a very dangerous bike. Riders often flew over the handlebars and suffered many injuries.

In response to the dangerous Ordinary, many "safety" bicycles were developed in the 1880s. The seat was placed lower and between the two wheels, making it much easier to balance.

Ending
Over the years many other changes were made to the bicycle. Lighter weight materials, better design, and experience have made the pastime of bike riding a popular, much safer activity today.

USE THIS SKILL

Write a Report

Choose one of the topics below. Then write a report about the topic.

Bicycle Topics

Bicycle safety
Mountain biking
Tour de France
Recumbent bicycles
Bicycle "spinning classes"

TEST TIP
You may be asked to write an extended answer on a test. You should organize your answer in the same way you would a report—with a beginning, middle, and ending. You should also support your main ideas with details.

Skill 30
HOW TO
Prepare a Display

Telescopes

For centuries people have enjoyed gazing at the stars and planets. The telescope has helped us learn much about our solar system.

A **telescope** is a tool that makes it easier to see objects that are far away. There are two types of telescopes: refracting and reflecting. The first telescopes were refracting. Refracting telescopes use two lenses to bend light. At one end of the telescope is the larger lens called the objective lens. A smaller eyepiece lens is found at the other end of the telescope. This is the lens through which a person looks. The objective lens gathers the light from a distant object and refracts, or bends, the light. The image that is formed is called the "real" object. It appears upside-down. Light from this image passes through the eyepiece lens. The light is refracted again and becomes parallel. The eye cannot tell that the light has been refracted. The faraway object looks bigger.

To learn more about telescopes, you can gather facts from books, the Internet, or from other people. You might also build a model or do an experiment to answer some of your questions about telescopes. To show what you learned, you can make a display. A **display** is an interesting arrangement of information you want to share.

A display is usually made of three panels placed together so they stand up. On the first panel, write what you wanted to know. In the middle panel, you should include your title and interesting visuals, or things to look at. On the last panel, record what you found out. Use the steps on the following pages to help you make a display.

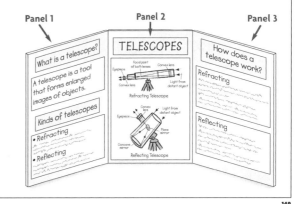

STEPS IN Preparing a Display

1 Choose a Topic

Pick a project topic that interests you. Ask yourself what you want to learn or what problem you want to solve. Start with one of these questions:

I wonder why . . .
I wonder what would happen if . . .
I wonder how that works . . .

2 Gather Information

The information you need to gather will depend on your project. If you built a model, you need to explain how it works. If you conducted an investigation, you will need to write the materials you used and the results of your experiment. For library research topics, gather facts from sources such as science books. Take notes on information to put in the display.

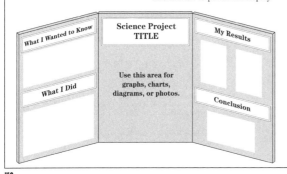

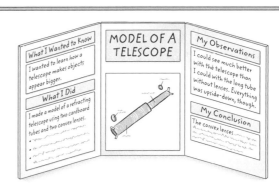

3 Get Organized

Make a plan for where to put your information on the display. Divide your information into sections to make your display easy to read. Your teacher may tell you what sections to use. Write a title and headings for each section. You can handwrite these or type them. Make sure they are neat and easy to read.

Under each heading, include only the most important information. Put this information on separate sheets of paper. Include drawings, photos, or charts. Each picture needs a caption to explain it.

4 Come to a Conclusion

In the last section, describe what you learned. Tell why the project was useful for you.

EXAMPLE OF Preparing a Display

Abby did an experiment with hand lenses to make a telescope. Look at her display below.

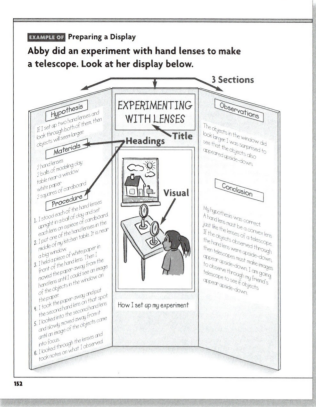

USE THIS SKILL

Prepare a Display

Make a display about one of the science topics below.

Science Topics
- Electricity
- The carbon cycle
- Weather
- Classifying rocks
- Vitamins and minerals
- Photosynthesis
- Magnets
- Gravity
- Plant and animal adaptations
- Earth and the moon
- Chemical substances

TEST TIP Some tests ask you to tell about what you have learned or what you think by writing an essay. Be sure your essay is organized so it has a beginning, a middle, and an end. Keep related ideas in the same paragraph.

Skill 31

HOW TO
Do a Survey

Cleaning Up the Environment

Weeds are growing in an empty lot next to Hawthorne Elementary School. The fourth-grade students decide they want to clean up the lot and turn it into a beautiful place.

The students decide to do a survey of the neighbors to see how they think the land should be used. A **survey** is a way to collect data by asking questions and then tallying the results. Use the steps on the next page to help you do a survey.

STEPS IN Doing a Survey

1 Decide the Purpose

First you must decide the purpose of the survey. Think about what you need to find out. The students at Hawthorne Elementary want to find out how most students and neighbors want the empty lot to be used.

2 Write Questions

A survey uses questions to gather data. Brainstorm a list of questions to ask people. Then choose the best questions. Leave out any questions that simply state a question in a different way.

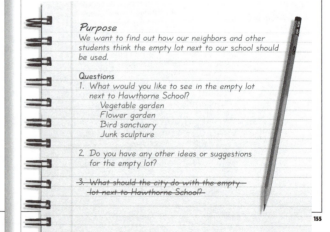

3 Ask Questions

You will want to ask many people your questions. If you ask only a few people, you won't have a very good idea of what most people think. As you ask people the questions on your survey, you can mark their votes on the sheets with tally marks.

Tallies are an easy way to mark and count votes. One line in a tally equals one vote. A tally that looks like this 𝍤 equals five votes. Tallies are easy to count because they can be counted by 5s.

First teams of Hawthorne students surveyed all the students in the school. Then they surveyed each block in the neighborhood.

Survey — Tom and Sue
1. What would you like to see in the empty lot next to Hawthorne school?
   Vegetable garden 𝍤
   Flower garden 𝍤 ||
   Bird sanctuary 𝍤 𝍤 𝍤
   Junk sculpture park ||||
2. Do you have any other ideas or suggestions for the empty lot?
   Playground
   Baseball diamond

Survey — Toshi and Mary
1. What would you like to see in the empty lot next to Hawthorne school?
   Vegetable garden |||
   Flower garden |
   Bird sanctuary 𝍤 ||
   Junk sculpture park ||
2. Do you have any other ideas or suggestions for the empty lot?
   Wildlife preserve
   Ice-skating rink
   Petting zoo
   Skateboard park
   After-school art shack
   Carnival

4 Show the Results

Once you have asked enough people the questions in your survey, you should show the results in a way that is easy to read and understand. One good way to show the results is by making a bar graph. The bars are easier to compare than tally marks.

TIP If you decide to use a graph to show the results of your survey, consider using a computer graphing program to make the graph.

The Hawthorne students made this bar graph to show their results. Each rectangle on the graph stands for five votes (or tally marks) on the survey. You can see that the flower garden got the most votes.

Idea	Number of votes (0–40)
Vegetable garden	▇▇▇▇▇
Flower garden	▇▇▇▇▇▇▇
Bird sanctuary	▇▇▇▇
Junk sculpture park	▇

EXAMPLE OF Doing a Survey

The students did another survey to decide which kinds of flowers to plant in the garden. Look at their data and bar graph below.

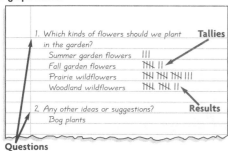

1. Which kinds of flowers should we plant in the garden? — **Tallies**
   Summer garden flowers |||
   Fall garden flowers 𝍤 ||
   Prairie wildflowers 𝍤 𝍤 𝍤 |||
   Woodland wildflowers 𝍤 𝍤 ||
2. Any other ideas or suggestions? — **Results**
   Bog plants

Questions

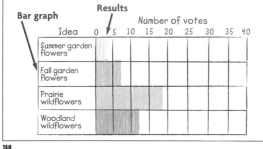

Bar graph — **Results**

Idea	Number of votes (0–40)
Summer garden flowers	▇
Fall garden flowers	▇▇
Prairie wildflowers	▇▇▇▇
Woodland wildflowers	▇▇▇

USE THIS SKILL

Do a Survey

Do a survey of your classmates to find out which environmental projects they prefer. You can use the list of ideas below to help you. Show the results of your survey in a bar graph.

Ideas for an Environmental Project

- Collect cans, bottles, paper, and plastic for recycling
- Save unwanted classroom papers to use as scratch paper
- Pick up trash on the school grounds or in a nearby park
- Host a "What's One Person's Trash Is Another Person's Treasure" sale
- Make posters urging students to buy recycled products
- Start a campaign to get your school to buy recycled paper

TEST TIP You might be asked to read the results of a survey on a bar graph when taking a test. Remember that longer bars stand for larger numbers and shorter bars stand for smaller numbers.

Skill 32
HOW TO Read a Time Line

Rockets!

"Five, four, three, two, one, . . . we have liftoff!" Perhaps you've heard this countdown before a space shuttle leaves a launch pad. The rocket science that allows astronauts to travel into space began thousands of years ago.

One way to see how rocket technology has changed over the years is to read a time line. A **time line** is a type of diagram. It lists dates and events along a line in the order they happened.

Time lines written across a page are read from left to right. The earliest dates are placed at the left of the time line. More recent dates are found toward the right side. Other time lines are written vertically (up and down) on a page. Use the following steps to help you read time lines.

Rocketry Around the World from 1200 to 1900

- **1241** Europeans begin rocket experiments.
- **1268** Arabs use rockets against enemies.
- **1232** Chinese use the first true rockets called "fire-arrows."
- **1379** First recorded use of rockets in European warfare.

STEPS IN Reading a Time Line

1 Read the Title
The title tells what the time line shows. The title may tell what time period is being shown. Some time lines have a theme, such as "American Rocket Launches."

2 Notice How Time Is Divided
Find out if the time is being measured in hours, days, months, or years. The time line below is divided into periods of one hundred years.

3 Look for Events
• Look at the order in which the events took place. Sometimes earlier events cause later events to happen. Knowing the order of events on a time line can help you understand relationships between events.

• Look at the distance between events on the time line. The distance gives you an idea of how much time passed between events. On the time line below, 21 years passed between the time that soldiers used rockets in the Civil War and the discovery that rockets work in a vacuum.

- **1650** Russians add fins to rockets.
- **1720** Dutch build model cars propelled by jets of steam.
- **1844** British build first rotary rocket with a fan.
- **1862** Soldiers use rockets during U.S. Civil War.
- **1687** Isaac Newton writes about the principle of action-reaction. Rocketry becomes a science.
- **1812–1814** British use rockets against Americans.
- **1883** Russians discover that rockets will work in a vacuum in space.

EXAMPLE OF Reading a Time Line

Read the time line below. Notice the order of events and how much time passed between each.

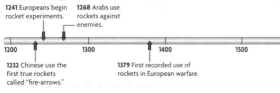

American Rockets and First Launch Dates

- **1956** *Jupiter C* — Tested nose-cone materials
- **1958** *Vanguard* — First attempts to put satellite into orbit
- **1959** *Atlas* — Important intercontinental ballistic missile (ICBM) with long-range capabilities
- **1961** *Mercury-Redstone* — Took Ham, a chimpanzee, and later Alan Shepard, the first American astronaut, into space
- **1962** *Delta* — Improved guidance and electronics of launchers
- **1966** *Titan III* — Used to put military payloads into space
- **1968** *Saturn V* — Eventually carried astronauts to the moon
- **1981** Space Shuttle *Columbia* — First use of both liquid and solid propellant; used reusable parts
- **1990** Space Shuttle *Discovery* — Launched Hubble Space Telescope

USE THIS SKILL
Read a Time Line

Read the time line below. Use the information on the time line to answer the questions.

U.S. and Soviet Union Launch Rockets to Carry Satellites into Space

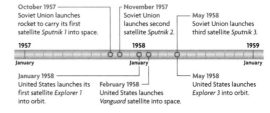

- **October 1957** Soviet Union launches rocket to carry its first satellite *Sputnik 1* into space.
- **November 1957** Soviet Union launches second satellite *Sputnik 2*.
- **May 1958** Soviet Union launches third satellite *Sputnik 3*.
- **January 1958** United States launches its first satellite *Explorer 1* into orbit.
- **February 1958** United States launches *Vanguard* satellite into space.
- **May 1958** United States launches *Explorer 3* into orbit.

1. In what year did the Soviet Union launch its first satellite into space?

2. How many months after the Soviet Union launched *Sputnik 1* did the United States launch its first satellite into orbit?

TEST TIP Some tests may ask you to tell the order in which events happened on a time line. Look to see where the time line begins and ends. Compare the dates from one end of the time line to the other to make sure you know which event happened first.

Skill 33
HOW TO
Make a Table

Going, Going, Gone?

For years scientists have warned that whole groups of plants and animals are disappearing. While we have made progress in saving some groups, time is running out for many others.

Mountain gorillas are endangered.

When a group of plants or animals is in danger of disappearing, it is **endangered**. There are many reasons why this happens. When humans decide to use an area, the plants and animals do not have a place to live anymore. Pollution has poisoned some groups of plants and animals. Many animals are killed by humans for their skins or other parts of their bodies. In nature, everything is connected. What happens to one group of plants or animals has an effect on others. If certain groups of plants or animals disappear, animals that depend on them for food may disappear as well.

When looking at information about endangered species, you may need to organize it so that it is easier to read and understand. A table is one way to do this. A **table** is a graphic tool used to show information in an organized way. A table also makes it possible to compare information easily. You can use the steps on the next page to help you make a table.

STEPS IN Making a Table

1 Choose a Title

Look over your information. Think of a few short words to describe the information. Those words will be the title of your table.

2 Choose Headings

A table has rows and columns. Rows go across the table. Columns go down the table. Decide which category of your information should go in rows and which category should go in columns. Usually the rows name the items that will be compared. The columns give different information about each item. When you have decided how you will organize your information in the table, write a heading, or title, for each row and column of the table.

3 Draw Your Table

After you have written a heading for each column and row, draw lines between the rows and the columns to make the boxes for your table. Now fill in each box with the correct information.

4 Check Your Table

Look over your table when you are finished. Read it from left to right across each row. Then read it from top to bottom down each column. Make sure that you have put the right information in each box.

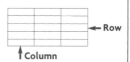

EXAMPLE OF Making a Table

Read the table below that shows information about the number of different animals living in the wild.

Headings   Title   Column

Endangered Animals			
Animal	Location	Number in Wild in 2001	Why Endangered?
Black rhinoceros	Africa	Fewer than 4,000	Habitat loss, hunting, poaching
Giant panda	China	1,000	Habitat loss
Mountain gorilla	Africa	Fewer than 650	Habitat loss, hunting, poaching
Northern right whale	North Atlantic and Pacific	Fewer than 1,000	Hunting (whaling)
Siberian tiger	Russia	450	Habitat loss, poaching

Row →

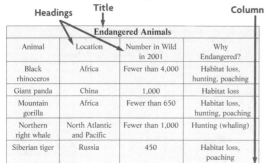

USE THIS SKILL
Make a Table

Use the information in the paragraph to make a table.

Numbers of Endangered Species

The U.S. Fish and Wildlife Service keeps track of the different groups of animals that are endangered. As of October 31, 2001, here are their numbers. A total of 314 species of mammals are endangered—63 in the United States and 251 in the rest of the world. A total of 253 species of birds are endangered—78 in the United States and 175 in the rest of the world. Of the 78 species of reptiles that are endangered, 14 are in the United States and 64 are in the rest of the world. A total of 81 species of fish are endangered—70 in the United States and 11 in the rest of the world. Of the 18 species of amphibians that are endangered, 10 are in the United States and 8 are in the rest of the world.

Animal Groups	Number of Endangered Species in U.S.	Number of Endangered Species in Rest of World	Total Number of Endangered Species

TEST TIP On some tests you will have to read information on tables. Remember to read straight across the rows and straight down the columns. Use your finger or your pencil to help you keep your place.

Skill 34
HOW TO
Read a Bar Graph

Up in Smoke

Today more people are making the choice not to smoke. They want to take care of their bodies and know that using tobacco is not a good idea.

Tobacco is a plant that contains the drug **nicotine**. Nicotine enters the body when a person inhales smoke from cigarettes, cigars, or pipes. Nicotine in the smoke goes into the lungs. It passes into the blood and goes to other parts of the body. Because a smoker's heart works faster and harder than it should, smokers are at a greater risk for heart disease. Tobacco smoke also contains substances that damage the lungs. Smoking increases a person's risk for getting lung cancer, as well as many other kinds of cancer. Many people who smoke would like to stop, but it is not easy to quit smoking. Most smokers become addicted to, or dependent on, nicotine.

One way you can find out more about the effects of smoking is by looking at a bar graph. A **bar graph** is a kind of drawing that compares two or more things. Each bar on the graph stands for an amount. Use the steps on the next page to help you read a bar graph.

STEPS IN Reading a Bar Graph

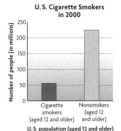

1 Read the Title and Labels

The title of the bar graph is usually found at the top of the graph. It tells you what kind of information the graph shows. The label along the bottom of the graph tells what kinds of items are being compared. The label along the left side tells what units were used to measure. Units might include the number of people, number of hours, or number of dollars.

2 Check the Number Scale

The number scale is usually found on the left side of the graph. The numbers will be written from smallest to largest, starting with zero. The numbers may be shown in ones, or in multiples of fives, tens, fifties, and so on.

3 Read the Categories

The categories name the things that are being compared. They are usually found at the bottom of the bar graph below each bar.

4 Compare the Bars

Find the longest and shortest bars. Look for bars that are the same length. If you need to know more detailed information, look for where each bar stops. To find where a bar stops, run your finger up the bar and across to the amounts.

EXAMPLE OF Reading a Bar Graph

Read the bar graph below that shows the number of deaths from diseases related to smoking.

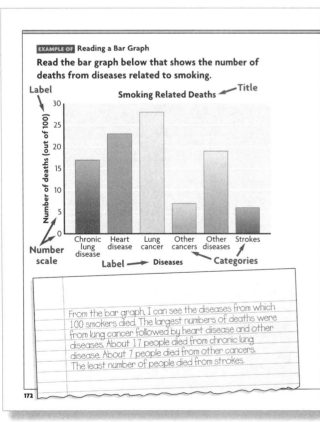

> From the bar graph, I can see the diseases from which 100 smokers died. The largest numbers of deaths were from lung cancer followed by heart disease and other diseases. About 17 people died from chronic lung disease. About 7 people died from other cancers. The least number of people died from strokes.

USE THIS SKILL
Read a Bar Graph

One hundred nonsmokers were asked why they choose not to smoke. Read the bar graph below that shows their answers. Then answer the questions.

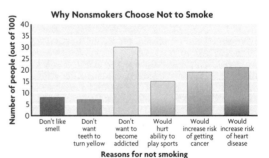

1. Which answer did the highest number of people choose for why they do not smoke?

2. Which answer did the lowest number of people choose for why they do not smoke?

TEST TIP You may be asked to read a bar graph on a test. Look carefully at the end of each bar so you know the value for which it stands.

Skill 35
HOW TO
Make a Line Graph

Tracking the Temperature

Mr. Rodriguez's class was studying weather. They wanted to find out how the temperature changed during the day, so they made a weather station. Every hour, the students measured the temperature. They recorded the temperature in a table.

Temperatures
February 3, 8:00 A.M.–3:00 P.M.

Time	Temperature
8:00 A.M.	20 °F
9:00 A.M.	22 °F
10:00 A.M.	25 °F
11:00 A.M.	28 °F
12:00 P.M.	30 °F
1:00 P.M.	35 °F
2:00 P.M.	37 °F
3:00 P.M.	40 °F

A table is a great way to record information. If you want to better understand the information or show the information in a different way, you can make a line graph. A **line graph** uses points, or dots, connected by a line to show how something changes over time. Look at the line graph below.

It shows how the temperature changed during the day on February 3. The bottom of the graph shows the time of day. The left side of the graph shows temperatures. You can see from the graph that the temperature became warmer every hour. Use the steps on the next page to make a line graph.

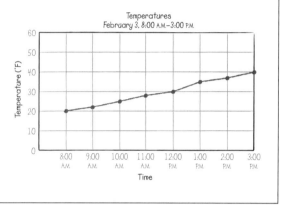

STEPS IN Making a Line Graph

1 Organize Your Information

Decide what information you want to graph. Then gather the information you need. You can organize your information in a table to make it easier to graph.

2 Draw the Graph

Use the data in your table to draw your graph. Usually the left side of the graph will show amounts. Amounts might include prices, temperatures, sizes of objects, or a number of people. The bottom of the graph will usually tell time categories, such as hours, days, months, or years.

First draw equally spaced lines going across and up and down to form a grid. Decide how you will show your amounts. Begin with a zero at the bottom left of your graph. Then look at the largest number in your table. Put that number at the top left. Now fill in the other numbers from your table. Put your time categories along the bottom of the graph.

Average High Temperatures in Millersburg	
Month	Average High Temperature
January	38 °F
February	42 °F
March	51 °F
April	58 °F
May	65 °F
June	74 °F

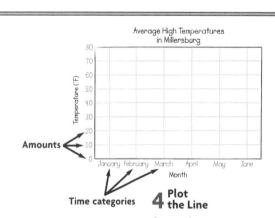

3 Add Labels and a Title

Add labels that name the amounts and time categories. Don't forget to include units of measurement if necessary. Be sure to include a title at the top of your graph.

4 Plot the Line

Once you have set up your graph, you can begin to plot your line. Place a point on the grid showing where the amounts for each variable meet. Then draw a line to connect the points.

TIP When making a line graph, use a ruler and a pencil to keep the lines straight. Neatly write labels to make the information clear.

EXAMPLE OF Making a Line Graph

The students in Mr. Rodriguez's class found out the average high temperature for each month in their town. Look at the line graph they made to show the information.

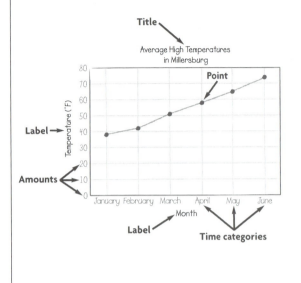

USE THIS SKILL
Make a Line Graph

The table shows the high temperature in Millersburg each day for one week. Use the table to make a line graph that shows how the temperature changed.

| Weekly High Temperatures in Millersburg ||
Day	High Temperatures
Monday	32 °F
Tuesday	35 °F
Wednesday	40 °F
Thursday	42 °F
Friday	37 °F
Saturday	35 °F
Sunday	30 °F

TEST TIP Some tests may ask you to read a line graph. Be sure to read the title to see what the graph shows. Then read the labels to see what units of measurement the numbers are in.

Skill 36
HOW TO
Read a Circle Graph

Conserving Water

Water is a natural resource that we need every day. We drink water and use it to bathe, cook, and clean. Farmers use water to grow crops. Firefighters use it to put out fires.

Earth has enough water to meet our needs, but the water is not always available when we need it. Pollution or drought, for example, might cause water shortages in some areas. Also, people who live in dry places, such as the southwestern United States, must get their water from miles away. If they use more water than can be brought in, they will have a water shortage too.

Because there is a limited supply of water, we must learn to conserve it. To **conserve** means to use less to keep something from becoming used up. During times of water shortages, people must limit their use of water. All unnecessary uses of water, such as watering the lawn or washing cars, may be banned.

Think of all the ways you use water in one day. The amount of water you use can be shown in a circle graph. Knowing how to read the graph might help you figure out how to use less water.

STEPS IN Reading a Circle Graph

A **circle graph** is a circle used to organize information. The circle is divided into sections. Each section shows a different part, or amount, of a whole. To read a circle graph, follow these steps.

1 Look at the Title

The title tells you what you will learn by studying the circle graph. Read it first so you know what the graph shows.

2 Read Each Label

Each section of the circle graph has a label. Sometimes sections of a circle graph have different colors or patterns to make the different sections of the graph stand out. Reading the label will help you figure out what part of the whole that section is. The sections will often be labeled with numbers.

3 Compare the Sections

Note that the sections are not all the same size. The sizes show different amounts or parts of the whole. The largest section of the circle graph represents the largest amount of the whole. The smallest section shows the smallest part. By comparing the sections, you will see how they relate to each other.

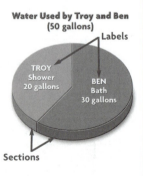

EXAMPLE OF Reading a Circle Graph

The table shows how much water Tracey used in one day. The table was used to make the circle graph. Study both the table and the graph to find out how much water Tracey used.

Washing Hands (5x)	Flushing Toilet (5x)	Brushing Teeth (2x)	Washing Dishes	Taking a Shower	**TOTAL**
3 gallons	7 gallons	1 gallon	12 gallons	20 gallons	**43 gallons**

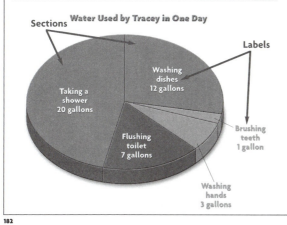

Water Used by Tracey in One Day
- Sections
- Labels
- Taking a shower 20 gallons
- Washing dishes 12 gallons
- Brushing teeth 1 gallon
- Flushing toilet 7 gallons
- Washing hands 3 gallons

182

USE THIS SKILL
Read a Circle Graph

Use the circle graph on page 182 to answer the questions below.

1. What does the circle graph show?
2. How much water did Tracey use when washing dishes?
3. How much water did Tracey use to brush her teeth?
4. Tracey washed her hands five times and used a total of 3 gallons of water. About how much water did she use each time she washed her hands?
5. If Tracey takes a shower once a day, how much water does she use in one week of showers?
6. During which activity did Tracey use the most water?
7. How much water did Tracey use in all?
8. What can Tracey do to conserve more water?

TEST TIP You might be asked to read a circle graph when taking a test. Pay attention to each part of the graph when you answer the questions. Be sure you are looking at the right part of the graph to answer the questions.

183

Skill 37
HOW TO Make a Diagram

Amazing Insects

Scientists estimate that there are as many as one million insect species in the world. That may seem like a lot, but many insects have not been identified yet. Every year about 7,000 new insect species are described.

Even though there are many different kinds of insects, they all have some things in common. Insects have bodies with three main parts and they have six legs. Instead of a backbone, insects have a thin shell called an exoskeleton on the outside of their bodies. Insects also have antennae that help them find out about the world as well as one or two pairs of wings.

Most insects do not start life looking like adult insects. An insect goes through great changes as it goes through its life cycle. Insects go through metamorphosis to become adults. **Metamorphosis** is when an animal changes body form and appearance during its life cycle. For example, you may know that butterflies don't start life as tiny "baby butterflies." They begin life as eggs and then go through the process of metamorphosis to become adults.

184

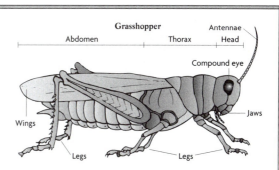

Grasshopper
- Abdomen
- Thorax
- Head
- Antennae
- Compound eye
- Jaws
- Legs
- Wings

You can make diagrams to help you understand science topics. A **diagram** is a graphic that is used to show and explain information.

A **picture diagram** uses pictures to show the parts of something or how something works. This picture diagram shows a grasshopper. The labels on the diagram explain the parts of the diagram. Pointer lines show where to look on the diagram.

Venn diagrams show how two things are alike and different. A Venn diagram is made of two overlapping circles. This Venn diagram shows how insects and spiders are alike and different.

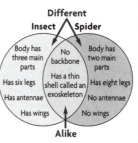

Different
- Insect / Spider
- Body has three main parts | No backbone / Has a thin shell called an exoskeleton | Body has two main parts
- Has six legs | | Has eight legs
- Has antennae | | No antennae
- Has wings | | No wings

Alike

185

143

A **line diagram** uses lines, words, and symbols to show how things or ideas are related. This diagram shows two kinds of metamorphosis—complete and incomplete.

Cycle diagrams show a process with no beginning or end that happens over and over. This diagram shows the life cycle of a butterfly. The arrows show how one stage of the life cycle leads to another.

Two Kinds of Metamorphosis

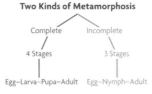

Butterfly Life Cycle

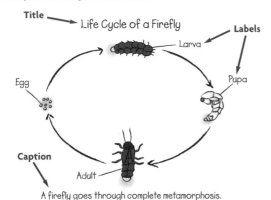

A butterfly goes through complete metamorphosis.

STEPS IN Making a Diagram
Use these steps to help you make a diagram.

1 Choose a Diagram

Think about what kind of information you have. Then choose a diagram that will work best to show and explain the information. Do you need to show the parts of something? Do you need to compare and contrast two items? Do you need to show how ideas are related? Do you need to show a cycle? Your answers to these questions will tell you what kind of diagram you need.

2 Draw the Diagram

Begin drawing your diagram with a pencil so that you can easily make changes as you work. You can use tools such as a ruler, a compass, or stencils to help you draw lines, circles, boxes, and other shapes. Include labels and pointer lines if you need to identify the parts of your diagram. Add arrows if you want to show movement in your diagram.

> **TIP** You can include a caption below your diagram if you want to provide more information about your diagram. A caption can be a few words or one or two sentences in length.

3 Add a Title

Add a title at the top of the drawing to tell the topic of the diagram.

EXAMPLE OF Making a diagram
Look at the cycle diagram one student made after reading about the life cycle of a firefly.

The Firefly Life Cycle

A female firefly lays eggs that glow in the dark. Soon a firefly egg hatches into a larva. The larva gives off light. After some time goes by, the larva becomes a pupa. The wings, legs, and antennae form during this stage. When it is fully developed, an adult crawls out of the pupal case. The firefly will soon be able to use its wings. It will eat, fly, and use its light to attract a mate.

Title → Life Cycle of a Firefly   **Labels**

Egg — Larva — Pupa — Adult

Caption → *A firefly goes through complete metamorphosis.*

USE THIS SKILL
Make a Diagram

Read the paragraph and look at the pictures. Use the information to make a cycle diagram.

The Dragonfly Life Cycle

A dragonfly goes through incomplete metamorphosis. That means that the life cycle of a dragonfly has three stages. The first is the egg. The eggs are very small. They are laid in large numbers in the water. The second stage is called the nymph. At this stage the dragonfly does not yet have wings. Nymphs live in the water and breathe by means of gills. As they near adulthood, they crawl out of the water and shed their shells. The third stage is the adult. The adult dragonfly has beautiful wings and spends much of its time flying.

Dragonfly eggs

Dragonfly nymph

Adult dragonfly

> **TEST TIP** On some tests you may be asked to read a diagram. Read the title to see what the diagram shows. Then use the diagram to answer the questions. Think carefully about what the diagram shows.

Skill 38
HOW TO
Read a Flowchart

How Storms Form

A storm rumbled overhead. Thunder cracked loudly and lightning lit up the sky. A heavy rain hit the ground.

Storms happen when two air masses meet. An **air mass** is a large body of air. Some air masses are cold. Others are warm. Air masses are slow to mix together because they differ in temperature, pressure, and density. They bump into or push against each other. The place where two air masses meet is called a **front.** Air masses also contain water vapor, or water in the form of gas. When a warm air mass and a cold air mass meet, warm air is pushed up into the colder parts of the atmosphere. As the warm air rises, it cools rapidly. This causes the water vapor to condense, or turn into small droplets of water. The water droplets form clouds.

To understand exactly what happens when two air masses meet, it is helpful to look at a flowchart. A **flowchart** is a drawing that shows a process or how something happens.

190

STEPS IN Reading a Flowchart

1 Read the Title

The title gives the flowchart's topic. It tells what the flowchart shows.

2 Follow the Arrows

Find where the flowchart begins. Then follow the arrows from step to step to read them in order. Finish reading one step before following the arrow to the next step.

3 Follow All the Paths

Sometimes the arrows will show you more than one path. Follow each path, reading the steps to see what happens in that path. Make sure to read all the different paths.

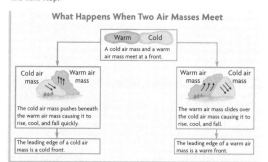

What Happens When Two Air Masses Meet

191

EXAMPLE OF Reading a Flowchart
Read the flowchart to find out how rainstorms, hailstorms, and snowstorms form.

Title → How Storms Are Formed

Beginning → Cold air pushes under a warm air mass.

← Arrow

The warm, humid air rises quickly into colder air.

As the warm air cools, water vapor condenses and forms a cloud.

- Droplets of water join together to form raindrops.
  - Raindrops fall from cloud as rain.
- Droplets of water freeze into balls of ice. Many layers of ice form on the balls.
  - The balls of ice fall to the ground as hail.
- Water vapor freezes into ice crystals called snowflakes.
  - The snowflakes fall to the ground as snow.

Ending

192

USE THIS SKILL
Read a Flowchart

Use the flowchart on page 192 to answer the following questions.

1. What does this flowchart show?
2. Where does the flowchart begin?
3. How many arrows do you count?
4. What are three possible results of a cloud, according to the chart?
5. How does a rainstorm form?
6. How does a snowstorm form?
7. How does a hailstorm form?

TEST TIP You might be asked to read a flowchart when taking a test. If the flowchart has drawings or photos, you can use them to understand the information. If the flowchart has words only, try to form a picture in your mind of each step as you read it. This will help you better understand what you read.

193

145

Skill 39
HOW TO
Make a Graphic Organizer

A Bright Idea

You may know about the inventor Thomas Edison. Have you heard of Lewis H. Latimer?

Lewis H. Latimer was an inventor too. He worked with Thomas Edison at Edison's New Jersey "invention factory." Beginning in 1878, Latimer experimented with a lightbulb that Edison created. Edison's lightbulb was made of a thin strip of paper that was attached to wires and enclosed in a vacuum inside a glass bulb. When electricity flowed into the paper, the bulb heated up and glowed. The lightbulb worked, but it burned out quickly. After many tests, Latimer replaced the paper with carbon, a more durable material.

To help you remember the facts you read, you can make a graphic organizer. **Graphic organizers** are lines and shapes that help you collect and organize information.

Lewis H. Latimer and the Lightbulb

Who?	What?	When?	Where?	Why?	How?
Lewis H. Latimer	Improved Thomas Edison's lightbulb	Beginning in 1878	New Jersey, at Edison's "invention factory"	Edison's lightbulb burned out quickly.	He replaced the paper in Edison's lightbulb with carbon.

5Ws and H chart

STEPS IN Making a Graphic Organizer

1 Choose a Graphic Organizer

After you read a passage, decide which type of graphic organizer will work best to show the information. To show the main ideas and details about a topic, try using a concept web. If you want to show the steps in a process, you can use a flowchart. A 5Ws and H chart is a useful organizer for recording the answers to the questions who, what, when, where, why, and how about a topic.

Concept web

2 Take Notes

Before you draw your graphic organizer, take notes on the passage you are reading. Jot down the most important information.

3 Draw and Write

Use your notes to help you draw your graphic organizer. Use tools such as rulers, stencils, and compasses to draw lines, boxes, circles, or other shapes. The way the information is organized will depend on the type of graphic organizer you use. Write words or short phrases. You do not have to write complete sentences. Be sure to give your graphic organizer a title.

EXAMPLE OF Making a Graphic Organizer

As you look at the flowchart, notice how it organizes the information in the paragraph.

How Today's Lightbulbs Work

Today an incandescent lightbulb has a coil of very thin tungsten filament, or wire, rather than the carbon that Latimer used. This filament is inside a gas-filled glass tube. When the bulb is on, electric current flows through the filament from one end to another. As the electrons that make up the electric current flow through the tungsten filament, they bump into the tungsten atoms. The electrons transfer energy to the tungsten atoms. This causes the tungsten atoms and the filament to get very hot. Some of this heat leaves the filament and can be seen as light.

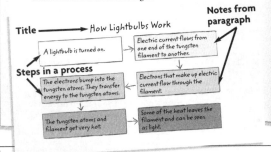

USE THIS SKILL

Make a Graphic Organizer

Read the passage below. Make a concept web to show the main ideas and details from the passage.

Energy-Efficient Lightbulbs

Only 10 percent of an incandescent lightbulb contributes to light. The other 90 percent is heat, which is wasted energy. For this reason, many people have replaced their incandescent lightbulbs with compact fluorescent lightbulbs. These lightbulbs cost more than incandescent lightbulbs, but they are more efficient and less heat is released. They also last up to ten times longer.

Compact fluorescent lightbulbs are made up of two parts: a gas-filled tube and a magnetic or electronic ballast that controls the flow of electric current in the tube. The gas in the tube glows with ultraviolet light when electricity from the ballast flows through it. To convert this light into light that can be seen, the tube is coated with a fluorescent powder. When the powder is exposed to ultraviolet light it absorbs the light energy and the light can then be seen.

> **TEST TIP** On a test you may be asked to write an extended answer. Making a simple graphic organizer can be a helpful way to organize your thoughts before you begin writing.

Skill 40
HOW TO Read a Map

The Everglades

Imagine a river of grass that is home to alligators, wading birds, and panthers. Believe it or not, this does not describe an exotic, faraway place. It describes the Everglades.

The Everglades, in southern Florida, is a wetland. **Wetlands** are low, flat areas of land that are covered with water most of the time. These areas are important for several reasons. Wetlands help control flooding, provide clean water, and are home to many kinds of wildlife. For many years, these areas were not protected. The land was drained and cleared. Some wetland areas disappeared as roads, homes, and farms were built. Many people argued that the wetlands should be protected. In 1947, part of the Everglades became a national park.

Maps can help us understand places like the Everglades. A **map** is a flat drawing that shows what a place looks like from above. You can use the steps on the next page to help you read a map.

STEPS IN Reading a Map

1 Read the Title

The title tells what the map shows. From the title, you can see that the map on page 198 shows the Everglades.

2 Study the Legend

The **legend** tells what the symbols and colors stand for in the map. The legend for the map of the Everglades includes symbols for cities and the state capital. You can also see from the legend that the land in southern Florida that is colored green on the map makes up the Everglades.

3 Look at the Compass Rose

A **compass rose** is a symbol that shows directions on a map. A compass rose usually shows the four cardinal directions: north, south, east, and west. Sometimes a compass rose shows only north. You can tell from the compass rose that north is at the top of the map on page 198. When reading a map, it is important to check the compass rose because north is not always at the top of a map.

4 Use the Scale

Maps include a **scale** that tells how distances can be measured on the map. The scale is a line marked in miles, kilometers, or both. One inch on the map might stand for 100 miles, 1,000 miles, or some other measurement.

EXAMPLE OF Reading a Map
See what one student learned from reading a map of Everglades National Park.

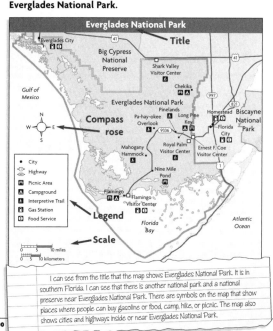

I can see from the title that the map shows Everglades National Park. It is in southern Florida. I can see that there is another national park and a national preserve near Everglades National Park. There are symbols on the map that show places where people can buy gasoline or food, camp, hike, or picnic. The map also shows cities and highways inside or near Everglades National Park.

USE THIS SKILL
Read a Map

Use the map on page 200 to answer the questions below.

1. What body of water borders Everglades National Park to the west?

2. What body of water borders Everglades National Park to the south?

3. In which direction is Big Cypress National Preserve from Everglades National Park?

4. How many miles is the Flamingo Visitor Center from the Shark Valley Visitor Center?

5. Name one place in Everglades National Park where camping is allowed.

6. Name one place in Everglades National Park where you can find a picnic area.

7. In which direction is Biscayne National Park from Everglades National Park?

8. How many miles is the Ernest F. Coe Visitor Center from Chekika?

TEST TIP You may be asked to read a map on a test. Begin by reading the title of the map to see what the map shows. Then skim the map. Look back at the map to answer each question.

Test-Taking Strategy
SKIMMING A PASSAGE

A mistake that many students make when taking tests is taking too long to read a passage. A **passage** is a short piece of writing, such as a paragraph or very short story. On a test you should **skim a passage.** This means you should read it quickly without trying to remember all the details. When you skim a passage, you just want to find the main idea of the passage.

Skim the paragraph below.

There are many types of living things on Earth. Birds, whales, lobsters, snakes, beetles, and trees are just a few of the organisms that live on Earth. Some species, or kinds of living things, have huge populations that get larger each year. Other species have tiny populations that get smaller each year. When a species has a population so small that it is in danger of dying out, it is called an endangered species. In 1973, the U.S. Congress passed the Endangered Species Act. This act protects endangered species and the areas in which they live. Since the act was passed, some endangered populations have recovered, or gotten large enough to survive. The gray whale is a species that was once on the endangered species list. Today its populations are large and stable enough that the gray whale was taken off the endangered species list. Although some species have recovered, many species continue to die out each year.

Answer the question.

1. What is the main idea of the paragraph?
   A. Gray whales are no longer on the endangered species list.
   B. The Endangered Species Act was passed in 1973.
   C. Bald eagles were once on the list.
   D. There are many endangered species that are helped by the 1973 act, but some species are still dying out.

How to find the answer:
When you skim a passage, you try to understand what the passage is mostly about. By just skimming the passage, you should be able to tell the main idea of the passage even if you don't remember the details.

- Gray whales were a small part of the passage. Gray whales were not the main idea of the passage, so answer **A** is not correct.
- The year that the Endangered Species Act was passed is a detail from the passage. You probably wouldn't remember this detail if you just skimmed the passage. Because it is a detail and not the main idea, answer choice **B** is not correct.
- Bald eagles were not mentioned in the passage. If you skimmed the passage, bald eagles probably wouldn't sound familiar. Answer **C** is not correct.
- Answer **D** describes what the passage is mostly about. By just skimming the passage, you can tell that this answer choice tells more about the passage than the other answer choices. Answer **D** is correct.

Test-Taking Strategy
UNDERSTANDING SEQUENCE

Sequence means the order in which things happen. A sequence question on a test will ask you about the order in which events happened. Sequence questions often ask you which events happened first or last. Answers to sequence questions can almost always be found in the reading passage.

Read the paragraph below.

A volcano is an opening in Earth's surface that can erupt, or send out gases, ash, and lava. Many volcanoes are active, which means they could erupt. What makes a volcano erupt? The simple explanation is pressure. Think about a soda can that has been shaken. The dissolved gases in the soda cause pressure to build up in the can when you shake it. What happens when you open the can? The pressure inside forces the soda to spray out. How is this like a volcano? Well, beneath Earth's surface, very high temperatures cause rock to melt. This melted rock, called magma, moves upward through cracks in solid rock. The dissolved gases in magma can form bubbles and build pressure within the solid rock. Like the soda forced out of a shaken can, pressure can force hot magma, ash, and gas through Earth's surface. Some volcanic eruptions are so powerful that they send clouds of hot ash high into the sky and across miles of land.

Answer the question.

1. Which of the following answers lists the events in the order described in the paragraph?
   A. gas bubbles form, pressure builds, volcano erupts
   B. shake a soda can, soda sprays, open the can
   C. volcano erupts, rocks melt, pressure builds
   D. open a soda can, shake the can, soda sprays

How to find the answer:
To answer the question, look for the answer choice that shows the events in the correct order.

- Answer **A** lists the events that happen when a volcano erupts. The order matches the paragraph, but keep reading to make sure there isn't a better answer.
- Answer **B** describes the events that happen when a soda can is shaken. Answer **B** does not match the order in the paragraph and is not correct.
- Answer **C** lists the events with the volcano erupting first. This does not match the order described in the paragraph. Answer **C** is not the correct answer choice.
- Answer **D** lists events about the soda can. Answer **D** does not match the order described in the paragraph and is not correct.
- After comparing the answer choices to the paragraph, Answer **A** is the best answer.

Test-Taking Strategy
MAKING COMPARISONS

Making comparisons is something you do every day. When you make a comparison, you tell how one thing is like another. A comparison always involves at least two things. Some test questions ask you to compare two things that you read in a passage. Other test questions may ask you to compare information from graphs, charts, or maps.

Read the paragraph below.

Imagine that you are walking through a park and you hear someone yell, "Watch out!" You turn to see a ball flying right at you. To keep from getting hit, you have to think fast and react to the ball. Like a reaction, a reflex can also protect your body from harm. When you touch something hot, your hand jerks away from the object before you have time to think.

Answer the question.

1. Which comparison is made in the paragraph?

    A. Your brain and nerves are alike.

    B. Information gets sent to the brain during a reflex.

    C. Both reactions and reflexes protect your body from harm.

    D. Reflexes are faster than reactions.

How to find the answer:
The question asks about a comparison. Remember that a comparison tells how two things are alike.

- Answer **A** is a comparison that tells that the brain and nerves are alike. Although the statement is a comparison, the paragraph does not compare the brain with nerves. Answer **A** is not correct.

- Answer **B** does not discuss two things. So answer **B** is not the correct answer choice.

- Answer **C** compares reactions and reflexes. It is a statement that tells how reactions and reflexes are alike. Answer **C** is probably right. Keep reading to make sure that the last answer choice isn't better than answer **C**.

- Answer **D** is tricky. If you weren't reading carefully, you might think answer **D** is the correct answer choice because it tells about reflexes and reactions. But this statement tells how reflexes are different from reactions. It doesn't tell how the two things are alike, so answer **D** is wrong.

- After reading all the answer choices, answer **C** is the best answer choice. It is the only statement that tells how the two topics in the paragraph are alike.

Test-Taking Strategy
SKIPPING DIFFICULT QUESTIONS

On a timed test, you want to answer as many questions as you can in the time that you have. The best way to do this is to skip questions that are difficult and come back to them later. Questions at the end of the test may be easy. You should try them before you run out of time.

Read the questions below.

Decide which one is easy and which one is difficult.

1. In the 1970s, the United States began working on a new kind of rocket-powered spacecraft called a space shuttle. It had three main parts that helped it move. The first part was an orbiter with three engines. The second part was a tank that contained liquid hydrogen and oxygen for the engine to use during liftoff. The third was two rocket motors that help provide thrust for liftoff. Based on the paragraph, what does thrust probably mean?

2. Scientists use rockets for research and exploration. Some rockets carry scientific instruments high into Earth's atmosphere. The instruments help scientists learn about Earth's weather and climate. Scientists also use rockets to send satellites into space. Satellites can take pictures of Earth's weather and gather many kinds of information. Rockets also carry astronauts and scientific instruments into space to gather information about objects in our solar system. Which of the following is **not** described as a way that scientists use rockets?

How to decide when to skip a question:

- Look at the length of the question. If you could answer three questions in the time it would take you to read one question, skip the longer question and return to it later. Both questions **1** and **2** are about the same length. Look to see if one question is more difficult than the other.

- Watch out for confusing words or numbers. Question **1** has many numbers. Each of the rocket parts described is made up of many pieces. This makes the numbers in the question confusing. Questions that seem confusing can take longer to read and understand than questions that are clear. Skip confusing questions. Question **2** does not have numbers and is easy to understand.

- Look for straightforward questions. Questions that are straightforward are easy to understand because they tell the question in a simple way that isn't tricky. Question **1** asks what the word *thrust* probably means. You cannot find the answer, so you have no way of knowing if your answer choice is correct or not. Skip questions that force you to guess which answer is correct. Question **2** asks you to tell which answer choice is not in the question. This means that you can check each answer choice with the information in the question. The answer choice that is not mentioned in the question will be correct.

- Question **2** is much easier to understand and answer than question **1**. On a timed test, it would be wise to skip question **1** and answer question **2**.

Test-Taking Strategy
USING KEYWORDS

Questions on tests often contain keywords. A **keyword** is a word that helps you find the correct answer by giving you an important detail. Keywords are often words that express time, such as *first, last, before, after,* or *during.* Keywords can also be words that compare two or more things, such as *larger, smallest, better, best, tallest,* or *heavier.* Any word that helps you find the correct answer to the question is a keyword.

Read the chart below.

LARGE EARTHQUAKES (selected)		
Year	Location	Magnitude
1906	San Francisco, CA	8.3
1923	Kwanto, Japan	8.2
1960	Chile	9.5
1964	Prince William Sound, AK	9.2
1976	Tangshan, China	8.0
1985	Mexico City, Mexico	8.1
1990	Iran	7.7
1995	Kobe, Japan	6.9
2000	Indonesia	7.9
2001	India	7.7

Use the chart to answer the question.

1. Which earthquake happened after 1995?

    A. The earthquake in San Francisco

    B. The earthquake with a magnitude of 8.0

    C. The earthquake with a magnitude of 6.9

    D. The earthquake with the same magnitude as the earthquake in Iran

How to find the answer:
The keyword in the question is *after.* You know the correct answer choice must have a date *after* 1995, not before or during that year.

- Find the year in the same row with San Francisco on the chart. The San Francisco earthquake happened in 1906. 1906 is not after 1995, so answer **A** is not correct.

- Find the year listed in the same row as 8.0. This earthquake happened in China in 1976. 1976 is before, not after, 1995. Answer **B** is not correct.

- Find the year that is in the same row with 6.9. This earthquake took place in Kobe, Japan, in 1995. That is the same as the year in the question, not after. Answer **C** is not correct.

- To find the year of the earthquake in answer **D,** you have to find the magnitude of the earthquake in Iran. You can see that the earthquake in Iran had a magnitude of 7.7. The other earthquake with a magnitude of 7.7 was in India in 2001. Answer **D** is correct.

Test-Taking Strategy
USING CONTEXT

When you read, there are times when you come upon a word or phrase that you don't know. This can happen on a test, in a book, or with anything else you read. To find the meaning of the new word or phrase, you can use the other words in the sentence or paragraph. The **context,** or the word's surroundings, can help you understand unfamiliar words or phrases.

Read the paragraph below.

For hundreds of years, people have made prosthetic body parts. Prosthetic parts replace body parts that have been damaged in an accident or by a disease. Long ago, prosthetic legs, arms, and hands were made out of wood or iron. Today prosthetic parts are made of high-tech materials. Hearts, hips, jaws, legs, and arms are just a few of the prosthetic parts made for the human body. These parts use plastics, ceramics, metals, and other materials to do the job of the body part they are replacing. Prosthetic body parts have changed a lot over time. Each year, doctors and scientists are finding new ways to improve the design, function, and comfort of artificial parts.

Answer the question.

1. Based on the paragraph, what does the word prosthetic mean?

    A. disease   C. damaged

    B. artificial   D. plastic

How to find the answer:
Even if you don't know what the word *prosthetic* means, you can figure it out from the passage. Find a place in the passage where the word *prosthetic* is used. Then replace the word *prosthetic* with the word in each answer choice. Find the word that works best in the sentence and keeps the meaning of the passage the same.

- Answer **A** is *disease.* Replace the word *prosthetic* with *disease* in a sentence. For example: Today *disease* parts are made of high-tech materials. This sentence does not make sense. Answer **A** is not correct.

- Answer **B** is *artificial.* Use this word to replace *prosthetic*: Today *artificial* parts are made of high-tech materials. This sentence makes sense and seems to have the same meaning as the word *prosthetic.* This answer choice may be right. Keep reading to see if there is a better answer.

- Answer **C** is *damaged.* Use *damaged* to replace *prosthetic*: Today *damaged* parts are made of high-tech materials. This sentence doesn't make sense. Answer **C** is not correct.

- Answer **D** is *plastic.* Replace *prosthetic* with *plastic*: Today *plastic* parts are made of high-tech materials. At first, *plastic* may seem to mean the same thing as *prosthetic* because some prosthetic parts are made of plastic. But the paragraph tells that prosthetic parts are made of many kinds of materials, including ceramics and metals. Answer **D** is not correct.

- The best answer choice is answer **B.** The word *artificial* is the word that most closely matches the meaning of *prosthetic.*

Test-Taking Strategy
WORKING CAREFULLY

When you take a test, it's easy to get nervous. You can make mistakes when you are nervous if you don't work carefully to answer the questions. When you work carefully, you read the details of the questions and take steps that will help you find the correct answer.

Read the paragraph below.

Many kinds of life depend on coral reefs. Coral reefs are formed by tiny animals called corals. When corals grow, they form limestone skeletons that can join with other coral skeletons. When corals die, their skeletons remain and other corals grow on top of them. A coral reef is a large group of corals living on the joined skeletons of millions of ancient coral. Coral reefs provide food and shelter for many kinds of ocean life. In fact, coral reefs are home to one of every four known types of ocean life. Coral reefs also provide food for millions of people. Whole cultures of people and many types of ocean life depend on coral reefs for survival. But many coral reefs are in danger. Pollution, overfishing, and the use of chemicals and explosives to catch reef fish are destroying large areas of coral reefs.

Answer the question.

1. Which of the following is not described in the paragraph?
   A. How many living things depend on coral reefs
   B. How coral reefs form
   C. What can harm coral reefs
   D. How people are protecting coral reefs

How to find the answer:

The key to answering the question is working carefully. Read the details of the question. The question asks you to find the answer choice that is not in the paragraph. The word *not* is a detail that will help you find the correct answer. You know that the correct answer will not be in the paragraph. By comparing each answer choice to the paragraph, you can find the correct answer.

- The paragraph says that many living things depend on coral reefs. Answer **A** is not the correct answer.
- The paragraph describes how coral reefs form. Answer **B** is in the paragraph so answer **B** is not correct.
- The paragraph lists a few of the things that can harm coral reefs. Answer **C** is not correct.
- The paragraph does not discuss how people are protecting coral reefs. Answer **D** is the correct answer choice.

Test-Taking Strategy
USING LOGIC

When you take a test, there may be some questions that ask you to find an answer when all the information is not given, or you have to estimate an answer. When this happens, you should think your way through the question by using logic. **Logic** is another word for thinking correctly.

Look at the chart below.

THE WORLD'S DESERTS		
Desert	Location	Area (square miles)
Sahara	North Africa	3,500,000
Gobi	Mongolia-China	500,000
Great Sandy	Australia	150,000
Great Victoria	Australia	150,000

Answer the question.

1. The Kalahari Desert is almost half the size of the Gobi. It is more than 70,000 miles larger than the Great Sandy and Great Victoria deserts. Which of these is the best estimate of the area of the Kalahari Desert?

   A. 700,000 square miles
   B. 120,000 square miles
   C. 225,000 square miles
   D. 3,600,000 square miles

How to find the answer:

In this question, you are given enough information to find the answer, but you still must use logic and estimate. An estimate is a guess that is based on information in a passage, graph, or chart. Sometimes an estimate is based on information you already know.

- Answer **A** is 700,000 square miles. This is larger than the Gobi, and you know that the Kalahari Desert is smaller than the Gobi. Answer **A** is not correct.
- Answer **B** is 120,000 square miles. This is smaller than the Gobi, but it is also smaller than the Great Sandy and Great Victoria deserts. You know that the Kalahari Desert is larger than these deserts. Answer **B** is not correct.
- Answer **C** is 225,000 square miles. This is smaller than the Gobi and larger than the Great Sandy and Great Victoria deserts. This may be the correct answer, but keep looking to see if there is an even better answer.
- Answer **D** is 3,600,000 square miles. This is much larger than the Gobi and is even larger than the Sahara, so it cannot be correct. Answer **D** is not the correct answer.
- After reviewing the answer choices, answer **C** is the correct answer. By using logic, you know it is the best estimate of the area of the Kalahari Desert.

Credits

Cover, Francois Gohier/Photo Researchers, Inc., (background) Ralph A. Clevenger/Corbis; **4** ©David Weintraub/Photo Researchers, Inc.; **6** (l) Matt Meadows, (r) David Parker/Science Photo Library/Photo Researchers, Inc.; **7** First Image; **8** Robert Brenner/PhotoEdit; **9** (t) Spencer Grant/PhotoEdit, (b) David Young-Wolff/PhotoEdit; **11, 12** Matt Meadows; **14** Alan & Linda Detrick/Photo Researchers, Inc.; **18** Matt Meadows; **23** AFP/Corbis; **26** Matt Meadows; **28** David Young-Wolff/PhotoEdit; **31** Matt Meadows; **32** Runk/Schoenberger from Grant Heilman Photography, Inc.; **38** Courtesy of Mote Marine Laboratory, Sarasota, Florida; **41** Jeff Rotman/Photo Researchers, Inc.; **42** Michael Newman/PhotoEdit; **43** Noble Proctor/Photo Researchers, Inc.; **60** ©Liane Enkeels/Stock Boston; **62** ©Mickey Gibson/Animals Animals; **63** Australian Picture Library/Corbis; **66** ©Mickey Gibson/Animals Animals; **69** ©John Bova/Photo Researchers, Inc.; **72, 75** AP/Wide World Photos; **82** Philip & Karen Smith/Stone; **84** Jack Dermid/Photo Researchers, Inc.; **85** C. Allan Morgan/Peter Arnold, Inc.; **87** ©John Serrao/Photo Researchers, Inc.; **90** James Shaffer/PhotoEdit; **94** Cobalt Productions; **100** ©WHOI-D. Foster/Visuals Unlimited; **104** David Boyle/Earth Scenes; **105** AP Wide World Photos; **106** Raymond Gehman/Corbis; **108** Jim Steinberg/Earth Scenes; **110** Still Pictures/Peter Arnold, Inc.; **114** ©CNRI/Science Photo Library/Photo Researchers, Inc.; **118** ©Richard Herrmann/Visuals Unlimited; **121** Dave G. Houser/Corbis; **124** Wolfgang Kaehler/Corbis; **127** Tom G. Lynn/Timepix; **131** (l) ©Robert W. Ginn/PhotoEdit, Inc., (r) Dimitri Lundt/Corbis; **132** ©Macduff Everton/Corbis; **140** (l, tr) Breck P. Kent/Earth Scenes, (br) Joyce Photographics/Photo Researchers, Inc.; **142, 145** ©Bettmann/Corbis; **148** ©Tony Freeman/PhotoEdit; **166** ©A. Plumtre/Oxford Scientific Films/Animals Animals; **174** Matt Meadows; **180** AP/Wide World Photos; **184** ©Michael Lustbader/Photo Researchers, Inc.; **187** ©Fabio Colombini/Animals Animals; **189** (t) ©Oxford Scientific Films/Animals Animals, (c) ©E.R. Degginger/Animals Animals, (b) ©Stephen Dalton/Animals Animals; **190** Keith Kent/Science Photo Library/Photo Researchers, Inc.; **192** (l) John Wilkes/FPG International, (c) Robert Lubeck/Earth Scenes, (r) Phil Degginger/Earth Scenes; **199** ©Jim Zipp/Photo Researchers, Inc.

Answers to Skills Workbook

Skill 1: HOW TO Make and Use a Model

1. Answers will vary. Possible answers include: the rocky layers of Earth's crust on each side of a fault line, the direction that the blocks of rock move, and so on.
2. Answers will vary: Possible answers include: modeling clay, cardboard boxes, chalkboard erasers, wooden blocks, and so on.
3. Answers will vary. Possible answers include: you could use a model of a fault to show the direction that the blocks of rock would move, you could use a model to show differences in the different kinds of faults, and so on.
4. Answers will vary. Possible answers include: The model and a real fault could both have layers. The model and a real fault could move in the same directions. The model would probably not be able to show the strength of the forces along a fault or the effects of the movement along a fault.

Skill 2: HOW TO Measure

1. 22 °C
2. −12 °C
3. 34 °C
4. 40 °C
5. 16 °C
6. 28 °C
7. 0 °C
8. −10 °C
9. Students should color in the temperature in the thermometer up to 28 °C.
10. Students should color in the temperature in the thermometer up to −14 °C.
11. Students should color in the temperature in the thermometer up to 36 °C.
12. Students should color in the temperature in the thermometer up to 48 °C.

Skill 3: HOW TO Choose the Right Tool

1. C. Tape measure
2. A. Ruler
3. A. Ruler
4. B. Meterstick

Skill 4: HOW TO Make a Hypothesis

1. He observed that after he rubbed an iron nail on a bar magnet, the nail was able to attract metal objects.
2. He knew that magnets attract iron and some other metals. He knew that some magnets are natural and some are made by people.
3. What would happen if I rubbed other metal objects on a bar magnet? Would other metal objects be able to attract metal objects like the nail did?
4. Students' hypotheses will vary. The hypothesis should be written as an "if . . . then" statement that can be tested. It should be based on the information provided in the passage.
5. Students' tests will vary. Accept all reasonable answers.

Skill 5: HOW TO Collect Data

Students should organize the data into two tables.
1. Stella conducted five trials. Brent conducted two trials.
2. Stella used six people in her investigation. Brent used three people in his investigation.
3. Answers will vary. Possible answer: Stella probably got more accurate results than Brent because she conducted more trials and she used more people in her investigation.

Skill 6: HOW TO Control Variables

1. material plants are grown in (plants in soil versus plants in rocks)
2. Answers will vary. Possible question: Will plants grown in soil or plants grown in rocks grow taller?
3. Answers will vary. Possible answers: type of plant, height of plant, type of container, amount of sunlight, amount of water, and so on.
4. Answers will vary. Accept any reasonable answers.

Skill 7: HOW TO Design an Experiment

1. If a group of herbs is placed in the west window, then it will grow taller than another group of herbs placed in the south window.
2. Students' plans will vary. Accept all reasonable plans that would test the hypothesis. Students should include numbered steps.
3. Students' materials will vary. Their materials list should correspond to the numbered steps in their plans.

Skill 8: HOW TO Draw Conclusions

1. Answers will vary. Possible answer: Dolphins use touching to communicate.
2. Answers will vary. Possible answers include: Dolphin sounds are related to dolphin activities and behavior. The different sounds that dolphins make have meanings that other dolphins understand.

Skill 9: HOW TO Prepare an Observation Report

Students should complete *Skills Workbook* pages 17 and 18 to help them write their observation report. Students' reports will vary but should correspond to the notes on *Student Edition* page 47.

Skill 10: HOW TO Classify

Students should write the names of the levers in the correct places in the table. First-class levers include the seesaw and screwdriver. Second-class levers include the wheelbarrow and nutcracker. Third-class levers include the baseball bat and broom.

Skill 11: HOW TO Compare and Contrast

Students' T-charts may vary. Similarities include: They are both outer planets. Both planets are large. They are both composed of gases. They both have 22 moons. They both rotate rapidly. Both planets have rings. Both planets take a long time to revolve around the sun. Differences include: Saturn is farther from the sun than Jupiter is. Jupiter is larger than Saturn. Saturn's gases are not as dense as Jupiter's. Saturn has more rings than Jupiter and its rings are brighter. Jupiter revolves around the sun faster than Saturn.

Skill 12: HOW TO Determine Cause and Effect

Students' answers will vary. They should write three causes and effects in the chart. Causes and effects include: **Cause:** Fire creates thick, black smoke **Effect:** it can be hard to see and breathe **Cause:** Fires can also spread very fast **Effect:** you may only have a few minutes to escape **Cause:** For these reasons **Effect:** your family should make a fire escape plan **Cause:** It is important that everyone knows the plan **Effect:** so that you all escape quickly and safely **Cause:** Smoke rises **Effect:** You should crawl on the ground **Cause:** If your clothes catch on fire, do not run **Effect:** that will make the fire spread **Cause:** stop, drop to the ground, and roll **Effect:** To put out the fire **Cause:** that is dangerous **Effect:** Do not go back into your home or try to put out the fire yourself

1. cause
2. cause
3. effect
4. effect
5. effect
6. effect

Skill 13: HOW TO Tell Fact from Opinion

Students should underline at least two facts in the letter. Possible facts include:
Yesterday we rode in a big boat out to the Great Barrier Reef.
The reef is off the coast of Australia and is about 1,250 miles long!
We went snorkeling in one part of the reef.
I wore a mask with a snorkel attached and a life jacket.
The snorkel helped me breathe while I swam.
The mask allowed me to see everything underwater without getting water in my eyes. The life jacket helped me float.

I could see many animals up close.
I saw many kinds of colorful fish.
I also saw white, yellow, green, and pink corals in many different shapes.
When I was snorkeling, I saw a big reef shark.
It swam by me, but it didn't do anything.
After a few hours we had to get back into the boat and go back to land.

Students should circle at least two opinions in the letter. Possible opinions include:
We are having so much fun here in Australia.
Snorkeling felt like being inside an aquarium.
I think that corals are really pretty.
Sharks are my favorite fish.
I hated to leave the reef.

1. Fact
2. Fact
3. Opinion
4. Fact
5. Fact
6. Opinion
7. Fact
8. Fact
9. Opinion
10. Opinion

Skill 14: HOW TO Find the Main Idea

1. B
2. D
3. A
4. C

Skill 15: HOW TO Take Notes

Students should take notes on the passage.
1. A wind turbine is a machine that converts the energy of the wind into electrical energy.
2. Students' answers will vary. Accept all reasonable answers. The wind turns the blades of a wind turbine. The rotating blades turn a shaft that connects to a generator. The generator turns the wind power into electrical power.
3. Wind turbines may have blades like propellers or blades like eggbeaters.
4. Small turbines may be 30 feet tall with blades that are 8 to 25 feet in length.
5. The largest wind turbine is 20 stories tall and has propeller blades as long as a football field.
6. Wind farms can have thousands of turbines.

Skill 16: HOW TO Estimate

Students' tables will vary. They should record all the foods they ate during one day. They should include how many servings from each group they ate during the day.
1. Answers will vary. Students should write from which food groups they need to eat more servings.
2. Answers will vary. Students should write from which food groups they need to eat fewer servings.
3. Answers will vary. Students should explain how they can improve their diet.
4. Answers will vary. Students should plan a healthful meal that includes foods from all of the food groups.

Skill 17: HOW TO Predict

1. Students' descriptions may vary. Possible descriptions: A tree is growing on a hillside. Its roots can be seen above the ground. The soil seems to have eroded.
2. Answers will vary. Students should mention examples of their prior knowledge of erosion.
3. Students' predictions will vary. Possible prediction: Over time the tree will probably fall over because as the soil erodes more of the roots will be exposed.

Skill 18: HOW TO Infer

1. Answers will vary. Possible answers include: The boy is dressed in clothes for playing soccer. He has a soccer ball. He looks upset or worried. The man in the picture is wearing a lab coat and examining the boy's knee. It looks like they are in a doctor's office.

2. Answers will vary. Possible answers include: People can get injured playing sports. Doctors help people who are hurt or sick. It makes me unhappy when I get hurt.
3. Answers will vary. Possible inference: The boy was injured while playing soccer.

Skill 19: HOW TO Make a Decision

1. Answers will vary. Students should list goals they could accomplish by doing a science fair project.
2. Students should fill in the chart with the science fair project ideas from *Student Edition* page 93. Students' advantages and disadvantages will vary. They should list at least two advantages and disadvantages for each possible science fair project.
3. Answers will vary. They should choose one of the science projects from their chart.
4. Answers will vary but should be connected to the goals students listed.
5. Student paragraphs will vary but should reflect the information they wrote in the chart. They should explain the reasoning behind their decision.

Skill 20: HOW TO Work in a Group

Student's name and partner's name should be written down, as well as three other names.

Answers will vary. All lines on the plan should be complete. Tasks include: collecting leaves, drying leaves, getting library books, asking for an adult's help to press leaves in waxed paper, and labeling the leaves. Due dates that fit in a one-week time span should also be shown.

Skill 21: HOW TO Make a Learning Log

Students' learning log entries will vary. Their learning log entries should be a reaction to the passage about fish that live in the deep ocean. Students can include drawings, questions, definitions of words, ideas that interest them from the passage, and other reactions to the topic.

Skill 22: HOW TO Write a Paragraph

Students should complete *Skills Workbook* pages 43–44 to help them write their paragraphs.

Skill 23: HOW TO Write an Outline

Students' outlines will vary. They should include the main ideas and details from the passage.

Skill 24: HOW TO Write a Summary

Students should complete *Skills Workbook* pages 47–48 to help them write their summaries.

Skill 25: HOW TO Write a Description

Students should complete *Skills Workbook* pages 49–50 to help them write their descriptions.

Skill 26: HOW TO Write a Comparison/Contrast

Students should complete *Skills Workbook* pages 51–52 to help them write their comparison/contrasts.

Skill 27: HOW TO Write about a Process

Students should complete *Skills Workbook* pages 53–54 to help them write about a process.

Skill 28: HOW TO Use the Library

Students should complete *Skills Workbook* pages 55–56 to help them use the library.

Skill 29: HOW TO Write a Report

Students should complete *Skills Workbook* pages 57–58 to help them write their reports.

Skill 30: HOW TO Prepare a Display

Students should complete *Skills Workbook* pages 59–60 to help them prepare their displays.

Skill 31: HOW TO Do a Survey

Students should complete *Skills Workbook* pages 61–62 to help them do their surveys.

Skill 32: HOW TO Read a Time Line

1. History of Space Probes
2. 1962
3. 1967
4. About six years
5. Probes to Mars
6. 1971
7. *Galileo*
8. 1959
9. *Pioneer 10*
10. Cassini space probe launched.

Skill 33: HOW TO Make a Table

Students' tables may vary, but should include the following information.

Habitats	Animals that Live There
Hot deserts	Antelopes, camels, snakes, road runners, Gila monsters, coyotes, mice, bobcats, scorpions
Tropical forests	Parrots and exotic birds, leopards, baboons, iguanas
Grasslands	Kangaroos, giraffes, zebras, elephants, tigers, prairie dogs
Mountains	Yaks, eagles, snow leopards, bighorn sheep, mountain goats
Polar regions	Polar bears, arctic foxes, walruses, penguins
Oceans	Whales, dolphins, seals, octopuses, lobsters, many kinds of fish

Skill 34: HOW TO Read a Bar Graph

1. 10
2. Japan
3. Ethiopia
4. Fifth highest life expectancy
5. China
6. Australia, Greece, and Italy
7. 59
8. Answers will vary. Possible reasons for higher life expectancy include: healthy diet, childhood vaccination against disease, exercising more, and so on. Possible reasons for lower life expectancy include: unhealthy diet, poor living conditions, poor health care, and so forth.

Skill 35: HOW TO Make a Line Graph

1. 10:30 A.M.
2. 1:30 P.M.

Skill 36: HOW TO Read a Circle Graph

1. C. Irrigation
2. D. Domestic and Thermoelectric power
3. B. 19%
4. B. For domestic use
5. A. 84%

Skill 37: HOW TO Make a Diagram

Students' diagrams may vary. They should draw a Venn diagram with one circle showing facts about butterflies and one circle showing facts about moths. The overlapping space should include information about how butterflies and moths are alike.

Butterflies:
- Brightly colored
- Fly during daytime
- 15,000 kinds
- Larger wings, smaller body
- Knobbed antennae
- Rest with wings straight up

Moths:
- Dull in color
- Active at night
- 250,000 kinds
- Fatter body, smaller wings
- Antennae are not knobbed
- Rest with wings out to the side or against the body

Shared by both:
- Insects
- Lepidoptera family
- Eat plants
- Four stages in life cycle

Skill 38: HOW TO Read a Flowchart

1. How Tornadoes Form
2. 10 steps
3. Severe thunderstorms called supercells form in unstable air.
4. Winds blowing at different speeds from different directions
5. Low, hanging clouds
6. At the southwestern edge of a storm
7. Northeast
8. The tornado gradually shrinks.

Skill 39: HOW TO Make a Graphic Organizer

Students' graphic organizers will vary. They should make a concept web that shows the main idea and details of the passage.

Skill 40: HOW TO Read a Map

1. Alaska
2. southern part of state
3. about 70 miles
4. Gulf of Alaska
5. Copper River
6. Chugach National Forest
7. Prince William Sound
8. about 120 miles

Skimming a Passage
1. C
2. B
3. C
4. A

Understanding Sequence
1. C
2. B
3. A
4. D

Making Comparisons
1. D
2. B
3. A
4. D

Skipping Difficult Questions
1. C
2. C
3. A
4. C

Using Keywords
1. B
2. D
3. C
4. A

Using Context
1. D
2. C
3. D
4. C

Working Carefully
1. A
2. C
3. D
4. B

Using Logic
1. D
2. B
3. A
4. C